THE HISTORY AND ARCHITECTURE OF
CHETHAM'S SCHOOL AND LIBRARY

THE HISTORY AND ARCHITECTURE OF

Chetham's School and Library

Clare Hartwell

YALE UNIVERSITY PRESS
NEW HAVEN AND LONDON

All illustrations, unless otherwise stated, were kindly supplied by Chetham's Library

Designed by Emily Winter
Typeset in Adobe Garamond by SNP Best-set Typesetter Ltd., Hong Kong
Printed in China through World Print

Half-title page: Mouth of Hell mask
Title page: Bluecoat boys in the cloister yard, early twentieth century

Library of Congress Cataloging-in-Publication Data

Hartwell, Clare.
The history and architecture of Chetham's School and Library / by Clare Hartwell.
p. cm.
Includes bibliographical references and index.
ISBN 0-300-10257-7 (cl : alk. paper)
1. Manchester (England)–Buildings, structures, etc. 2. Architecture–England–Manchester. 3. Manchester (England)–History. 4. Chetham's School of Music. 5. Chetham's Library. 6. Chetham family. I. Title.
DA690.M4 H366 2004
727'.478'0942733–dc22

2003020947

To my husband
James Muir Morrison

Contents

1. Detail of Fig. 29

Acknowledgements

This book could not have been published without generous grants made by English Heritage, Mr Paul Minet, and by the Paul Mellon Centre for Studies in British Art. A grant towards the cost of illustrations was made from the Stroud Bursary, administered by The Society of Architectural Historians of Great Britain. The feoffees of Chetham's School and Library have supported this project from the outset.

My greatest debt with regard to research for this volume is to the staff of Chetham's Library, especially the Chetham's Librarian, Dr Michael Powell, who put the results of his own research at my disposal and helped with many aspects of the preparation of the text and illustrations. His knowledge of the library collections, helpful suggestions and encouragement have been invaluable. Dr Fergus Wilde, Senior Librarian, has been unfailingly helpful, especially in the preparation of illustrations. Special thanks go to the Chetham's Archivist Jane Foster, who made an important contribution to the book through her transcription of the seventeenth-century building accounts, and thanks go to Paul Booth for checking the transcription. Jane gave me invaluable assistance in the reading, interpretation and transcription of other records held in the archive. I am also grateful to Sue Little and all the other library staff.

My thanks go to the Bursar, Cyril Barratt, and the staff of Chetham's School, who gave me access to the building and assisted with arrangements for photography and taking dendrochronological samples. I am indebted to Professor Brian Pullan for his helpful comments on the text. Ian Tyers of the Sheffield Dendrochronology Laboratory and Martin Cherry of English Heritage helped me to gain new insights into the building, and Hannah Hartwell gave me the benefit of her expertise on seventeenth-century English carving schools. I am grateful to Claire Gapper for her comments on the plasterwork and to David Porter who made helpful suggestions concerning the silver. Frank Kelsall has been a supporter of the project from the beginning.

This book would not have been possible without the support of John Nicoll and Sally Salvesen of Yale University Press, and I am especially grateful to Emily

Winter of Yale who designed and edited the book. My thanks are owed to Judith Wardman who prepared the index.

All the colour photographs, unless otherwise indicated, were taken by Beccy Lingard of Positive Image Photography for Chetham's Library. Black and white photographs, unless otherwise indicated, are from the Library's J.J. Phelps collection of glass slides and lantern slides dating from the late nineteenth century. Maps, engravings and watercolours are from the Library's collections unless otherwise indicated. I am grateful to the Dean and Canons of Manchester Cathedral for their permission to use photographs of the Cathedral and to Greater Manchester County Record Office for permission to reproduce drawings by John Palmer.

Introduction

Chetham's School and Library is a remarkable institution occupying an equally remarkable building (Fig. 2). It originated in the early fifteenth century as a college of priests, the home of priests and choristers who officiated at the parish church (now Manchester Cathedral), and lived together under a warden. It was

2. The college building, erected in the fifteenth century and used by Chetham's School and Library from the mid-seventeenth century

3. The buildings seen from the roof of Manchester Cathedral. The original medieval college is flanked by the former Palatine Hotel of 1842, left, and the late nineteenth-century buildings of Manchester Grammar School, right

known as 'the College' or the 'College House', well into the nineteenth century, hundreds of years after the priests had left the building after the Reformation. Few establishments of this type survive, and this is the best and most complete example of its date in the country, of national importance both architecturally and historically.

Although the building lies in the centre of Manchester it is surprisingly easy to overlook. Taller nineteenth and twentieth century buildings hide it from view (Fig. 3), so only the north side, near Victoria Station, can easily be seen from the street, and even that is partially obscured by trees and classroom blocks. The area had become a slum by the nineteenth century, when Friedrich Engels described the area between the Irk and Long Millgate as containing 'unqualifiedly the most horrible dwellings which I have yet beheld'.[1] Even after clearances it remained a backwater until development at the end of the

4. Statue of Humphrey Chetham by William Theed, 1853. Reproduced by kind permission of the Dean and Canons of Manchester Cathedral

twentieth century, when a new park was laid out opposite the entrance and the area reintegrated with the centre.

In earlier times the college was one of the most prominent buildings in town. It was noted by many visitors, of whom John Leland in *c.* 1538 was one of the first to record his impression of the 'fair builded' college of priests.[2] The parish church had been lavishly rebuilt by wealthy local families and patrons, and the priests, their assistants (known as clerks) and choristers engaged in performing duties there, lived in the building which in many ways resembled large manor houses of the period, both in appearance and in the way it was run.

After the Reformation, when the college was dissolved, the building was sold to Edward, third Earl of Derby, and member of one of the most powerful of the old Lancashire families. One of the most famous residents was John Dee, the Elizabethan astrologer and mathematician, noted for his interest in the occult, who lived there at the end of the sixteenth century. During the Civil War the building was a centre of operations in the Parliamentarian defence against Royalist forces, part of it was used as a gunpowder factory and other parts as a prison. The college was sequestered from the Earl of Derby with the rest of his estates by Parliament, and for the first time the building faced a serious threat to its survival. Part of the complex was converted to form one of the first Baptist meeting rooms in the region, and the Baptist leader, a notorious radical, went on to acquire the whole building. Its future was not secured until it was bought by the executors of Humphrey Chetham's will in 1665.

The educational charity founded through Chetham's bequest created a school and library, reusing the fifteenth century college building. Although many changes have taken place, both continue to honour the intentions of the founder, and are testimony to the diligence of generations of feoffees, or governors, who have governed them. The school, then called a hospital, originally educated and cared for forty poor boys, and the library has been, in the words used by Chetham in his will, open to 'schollars and others well affected . . . as a publick librarie'[3] without charge ever since. It had acquired a reputation by 1670 when the Master of Jesus College, Cambridge, described it as: 'a fair library of books . . . better than any college library in Cambridge.'[4] Distinguished visitors, of whom the best-known are probably Karl Marx and Friedrich Engels, included Celia Fiennes, Daniel Defoe, Robert Southey and John Dalton. It is an important and early example of a town library with an exceptional collection of books and manuscripts, made the more memorable by the marvellous original furnishings.

For 350 years a combination of good stewardship, parsimony and respect for the ancient building has brought it into the twenty-first century little changed

from the time of its erection and substantially as Celia Fiennes saw it in 1698. She described:

> 'the Colledge, which is a pretty neate building with a large space for the boys to play in and a good garden walled in; there are 60 Blew Coate boys in it, I saw their appartments and was in the cellar and dranck of their beer which was very good I alsoe saw the kitchen and saw their bread cutting for their supper and their piggins [drinking vessels] for their beere; there is a Cloyster round a Court; in it is a large roome called a parlour and over it a roome for the Judges to eate in; there is a large Library 2 long walls full of books on each side . . .'[5]

There follows an account of the collection of curiosities to be seen in the library, which included a rattlesnake skin and a human skeleton. Fiennes was evidently very impressed; the passage on the College takes up by far the greatest part of her entry on Manchester.

5. The Chetham's brass band in 1896. The band was a regular feature of traditional Whit walks in Manchester during the nineteenth century

The number of pupils gradually grew over following centuries, and the sight of the 'bluecoat boys', so called for their distinctive charity-school uniform, became a familiar one in Manchester (Fig. 5). It was not until the twentieth century that substantial changes were made to the way in which the institution was run. As with most schools of this type the constitution was changed in line with the 1944 Education Act. In 1950 it merged with Nicholls Hospital, another Manchester charity school founded in the 1860s; and in 1952 it became a boys' grammar school with selective entry. Steps were later taken to change it into a specialist music school, the first of its kind in the country, and from 1969 the children were selected for their exceptional ability in music. In the same year the former Palatine Hotel, which had been put up on the west side of the site in 1842, was bought and converted, and for the first time girls were admitted

6. Christopher Saxton's Map of Lancashire, 1577

to the school. In 1978 accommodation was expanded into the late nineteenth-century buildings along the Long Millgate frontage which had been vacated by the Manchester Grammar School in the 1930s, and a new classroom block was built alongside them. The school changed its name to Chetham's School of Music in 1977 and it has developed a reputation as one of the foremost music schools of its type. Like the bluecoat boys before them, boys and girls use the fifteenth-century quarters of the priests and singing men, and meet together in the great hall for special occasions. The school is known affectionately as 'Chet's', in Manchester, although the proper pronunciation of the name Chetham is thought to have been with a long 'e' in accordance with early-seventeenth-century spellings of the founder's name, which he did not standardise to the present form until 1635. In practice both forms, with a long or short 'e' sound, are widely used.

This account traces the history of the site and of the building from its inception in the 1420s through to the incorporation of Chetham's charity in 1665. Appendices cover examples of comparative buildings, a description and discussion of the roof structure and of the nineteenth-century additions and alterations. Appendix 3 is a short note on tree ring analysis undertaken on part of the building. Appendix 5 reproduces the building accounts for 1656–8, which include detailed information on rates of pay, sources of raw materials, and the names of craftsmen and labourers. Other primary sources are listed in the bibliography.

CHAPTER ONE

A 'Fair Builded' College of Priests

Church and College in Medieval Manchester

John Leland's description of Manchester in the 1530s noted the 'Hirke river' and the college which 'standith as in the veri point of the mouth of hit. For hard therby it runneth into the Wyver [Irwell].'[6] This site, a rocky outcrop rising about forty feet above river level, has probably been occupied since the Norman Conquest, and quite possibly before. Commanding the confluence of the rivers Irwell and Irk, as Leland noted, and the line of the Roman road from Chester to Carlisle, the strategic importance of the position is no longer obvious, as the River Irk has been culverted and neighbouring street levels raised high above water level. The spot was chosen by the Grelley family, who acquired the land after the Norman Conquest, for their manor house. The house and its grounds are described in surveys of 1267 and 1320 and there is every likelihood that their castle, first recorded in 1184, stood in the same position.[7]

Archaeologists and antiquarians have identified three ditches running in an arc between the two rivers around the site, which effectively made it into an island. Fig. 9 shows a schematic representation of the layout of the late medieval town with the ditches in relation to the main medieval buildings. Part of the outermost ditch, a watercourse called Hanging Ditch, is crossed by a medieval

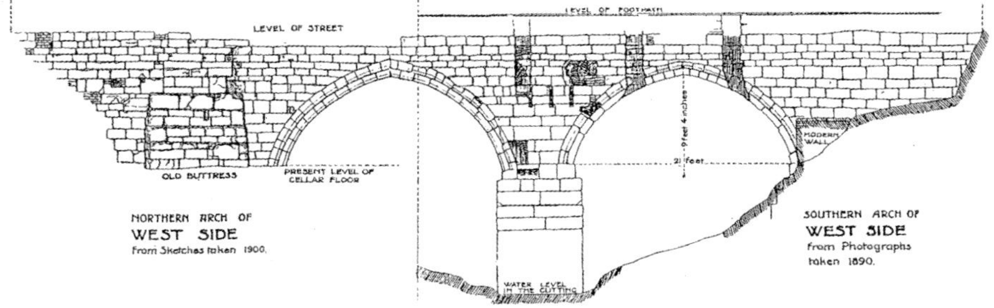

7. Mouth of Hell mask. Detail of medieval timber ceiling, Audit Room

8. Hanging Bridge shown in a drawing of 1904

9. Schematic plan of Manchester in the fifteenth century

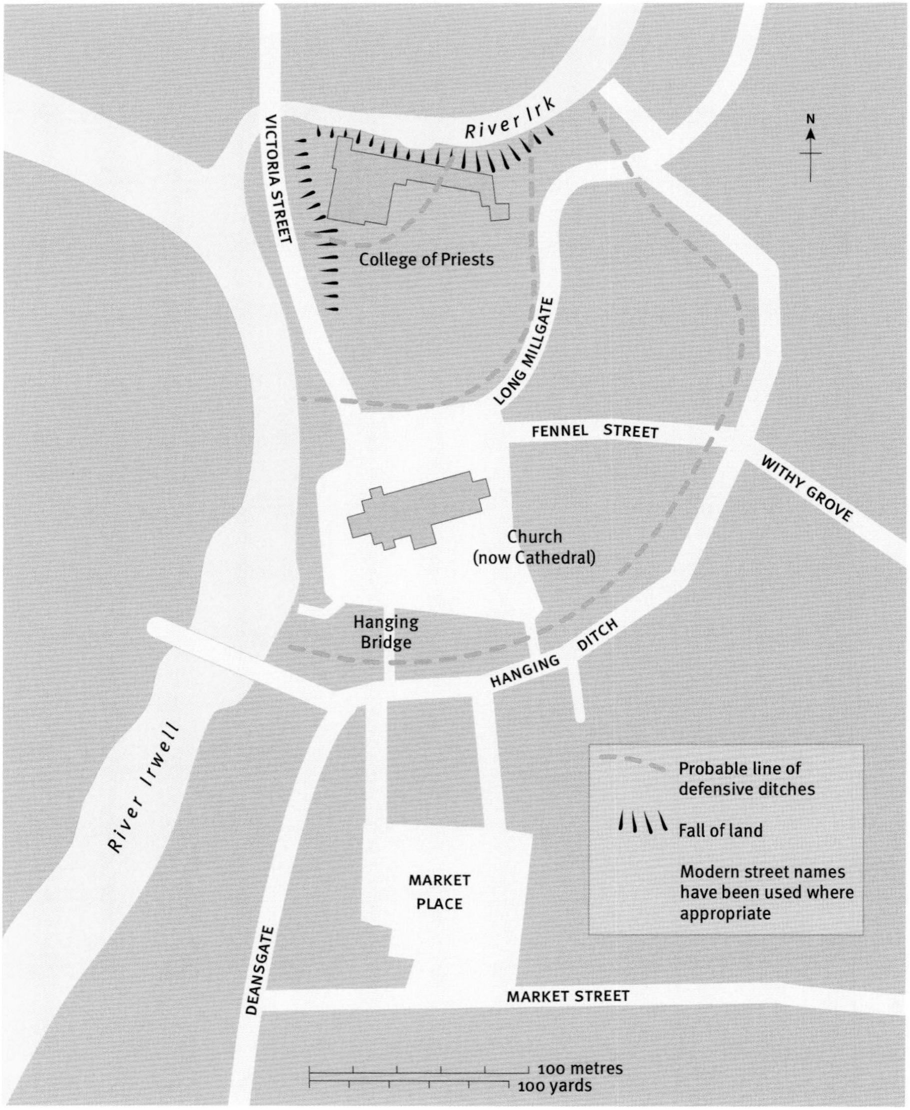

bridge which can be seen in the Cathedral Visitor Centre on Cateaton Street. Hanging Bridge crosses the ditch at a point where it is around sixty feet wide (Fig. 8). There are two Tudor arches, suggesting that it was probably built in the fifteenth century, perhaps when the church was being rebuilt. An earlier bridge on the site is mentioned in 1343, and there was probably a crossing place here for as long as a church has been on the site.

The ditch itself originated as a natural watercourse which was probably modified to improve its defensive capabilities, and the other two ditches are likely to have been created to make the site more secure. The second ditch,

10. Eleventh- or twelfth-century carving of an angel found during restoration of the Cathedral. Reproduced by kind permission of the Dean and Canons of Manchester Cathedral

which runs approximately along the line of Long Millgate, has been observed at various times by antiquarians, and a third, running through Chetham's School courtyard, was partially excavated in 1981.[8] The top of this can be seen at the foot of the wall between the college building and the Palatine Building, on the west side of the site. At the base, some nine to ten feet below the level of the courtyard, there is a shallow arch, over twenty feet wide, designed as a relieving arch to carry the wall over a ditch cut into natural sandstone. The excavation suggested that it may be as much as fifteen feet deep. Late medieval pottery artefacts recovered from the fill suggest it may have been filled in and capped at about the time of the establishment of the college in 1421.

The ditches have not been dated, but they were probably part of the defences of the Norman castle and may have even earlier origins. A fortified position or *burh* in Manchester is mentioned in the Anglo-Saxon Chronicle in 919 when Edward the Elder ordered that an army should occupy and repair it. No evidence for the re-use of the Roman Fort by the Saxons has been

11. The collegiate church, now Manchester Cathedral, shown in *The Builder*, 1893

found, so it seems possible that the Chetham's site formed the principal point for strategic defence of the area.

The medieval town grew up around the manor house, and the parish church (now Manchester Cathedral) was probably established at an early date, and may well be on the site of a church mentioned in the Domesday survey. The earliest surviving fabric seems to be of fourteenth-century date, though an eleventh- or twelfth-century carving of an angel was discovered during alterations (Fig. 10), which also produced evidence of thirteenth-century work. The church lies within the line of Hanging Ditch, and the present building (Fig. 11), 'one of the best examples of the [Perpendicular] style, with its spreading array of chapels, its grand tower, and exquisitely carved stalls'[9] is large and lavishly decorated, with superb late medieval furnishings, reflecting substantial rebuilding after the establishment of the college in 1421. Together the church and college buildings represent one of the largest and most complete examples of a late medieval collegiate foundation in the country.

The Manor of Manchester passed from the Grelleys to the de la Warre family in 1311, and Thomas de la Warre (*c.* 1359–1426) succeeded to the manorial rights in 1398 when he was already rector of the parish church. The rectors were appointed by the lords of the manor, or by the king if the lord was a minor, and rectors usually also held secular offices in the service of the lord or the king. Consequently they were pluralists and, often, absentees. As both lord and rector de la Warre was well-placed to bring about a reform in Manchester's ecclesiastical administration, which he did in 1421 when a licence to form a collegiate church was obtained from Henry V. The churchwardens and parish assented in the same year, and in August 1421 the Bishop of Lichfield granted a decree to make the parish church into a collegiate church.

The church continued to function as the parish church, but the way in which it was administered changed. Prior to collegiation it was possible for the rector to collect the income from tithes and to appoint another priest to act for him, leaving him free to take up other appointments and live elsewhere. Neglect of duties on the part of rector or his replacement could mean that the souls of the parishioners might be endangered, a cause for concern on the part of the authorities, as well as parishioners. An affecting story related by Eamon Duffy tells of the distress of a poor man in sixteenth-century Devon, whose arrangements for a requiem mass for his baby twins were disrupted by the absence of a clerk to assist the priest, providing a very human reminder of how this might affect ordinary people.[10]

The warden of the college took the place of the rector, and performed his duties, and he and the fellows were chantry priests, saying masses every day for Henry V, the Bishop of Coventry and Lichfield, Thomas de la Warre, and their forebears. Manchester conforms with the type of college characteristic of the later Middle Ages, in which the chantry priests were required to live as a community and to remain resident. A building was provided as a residence for members of the community, and the government of the church and the cure of souls were invested in the college.

The increase of chantries in the fourteenth and fifteenth centuries reflects the popularity of this form of benefaction in the later medieval period. In earlier times, wealthy individuals often founded or endowed monasteries, but this required enormous resources. The formation of a college such as that at Manchester was a formidable, if lesser enterprise, while founding a chantry was within the means of men without large fortunes. A chantry was an endowment to provide one or more priests to say masses for the souls of the dead, and, as in this case, the living. This was believed to help the progress of the soul through purgatory to heaven. De la Warre, the Bishop and the King had masses said for themselves and their progenitors in the expectation that this would continue after their deaths and assist their own progress to heaven. It was not unusual for a later medieval church to have numerous chantries which were often established in chapels built by the families who endowed them. In Manchester there were at least seven such chapels by the early sixteenth century.

The preamble to Manchester's charter of foundation makes it clear that in addition to the founding of the chantries, the large size of the parish and the abuses of previous rectors were reasons for collegiation:

> 'the aforesaid church of Manchester having a large and ample parish and very populous, had been accustomed to be ruled and governed in bygone times by rectors, some of whom never [and] some very seldom cared to personally reside in the same, – but that to the same church, over which a great and grand cure of souls did and doth hang, they [the rectors] caused the adminicle [aid, or ministry] to be served by the remotive [removeable], stipendiary chaplains, converting for their own pleasure the profits and revenues of the same church to their own uses, – from whose long absence followed a neglect of the cure of souls, a diminution of Divine worship, a defrauding of hospitality and of the support of the poor, and a great danger to souls.'[11]

The Charter of Foundation with the King's seal is preserved in the Cathedral (Fig. 12).

The new foundation consisted of a warden, eight priests or fellows, four clerks and six lay choristers. The income from the rectorial tithes was augmented by de la Warre, who gave lands in and around Manchester in 1422. Further grants were made to the first warden, John Huntingdon, by Reginald West, de la Warre's successor, over the period 1430–6.[12] The church, which had previously been dedicated to St Mary, was rededicated to SS Mary, Denys (patron saint of France) and George, perhaps because Henry's claim to the French throne had been strengthened by his marriage to the French King Charles VI's daughter in 1420. The church was enlarged and rebuilt during the fifteenth century, reaching its present size in the early sixteenth century.

Unlike a monastery the college members did not take vows, or live according to a particular rule, but collegiation helped to ensure that the lives of members were regulated so that duties were carried out properly and unseemly conduct and absenteeism reduced. Membership of the college was desirable for the status conferred, and also for the income. In 1534 the clear value of the college was

£213 10*s.* 11*d.* The warden received £20 a year and the eight fellows £4, leaving a substantial sum for other college members and for running and maintenance costs.[13] College appointments played a part in the web of late medieval political and ecclesiastical patronage, and in Manchester the powerful Stanley family, Earls of Derby, monopolised the wardenship of the college between 1481 and 1506 to promote family members and to ensure that their protégés succeeded to the office thereafter.[14]

Domestic arrangements in the college mirrored life in any large house of the period, just as the building in many ways resembled a manor house. As Mark Girouard explains it, 'The resemblance between houses and colleges is not surprising, for the colleges were founded by the owners of houses, who modelled both their organisation and their architecture on what they were familiar with.'[15] Some indication of the size of the household is given by the report of Henry VIII's commissioners in 1546, though the numbers of fellows, and probably also of servants, had been reduced by that time. The document mentions eleven officers in addition to college members. These were the warden's clerk, a butler, cook, 'horsekeper', brewer, baker and five 'ordinarie officers'.[16] A wealthy and well-born warden may have had a larger retinue of

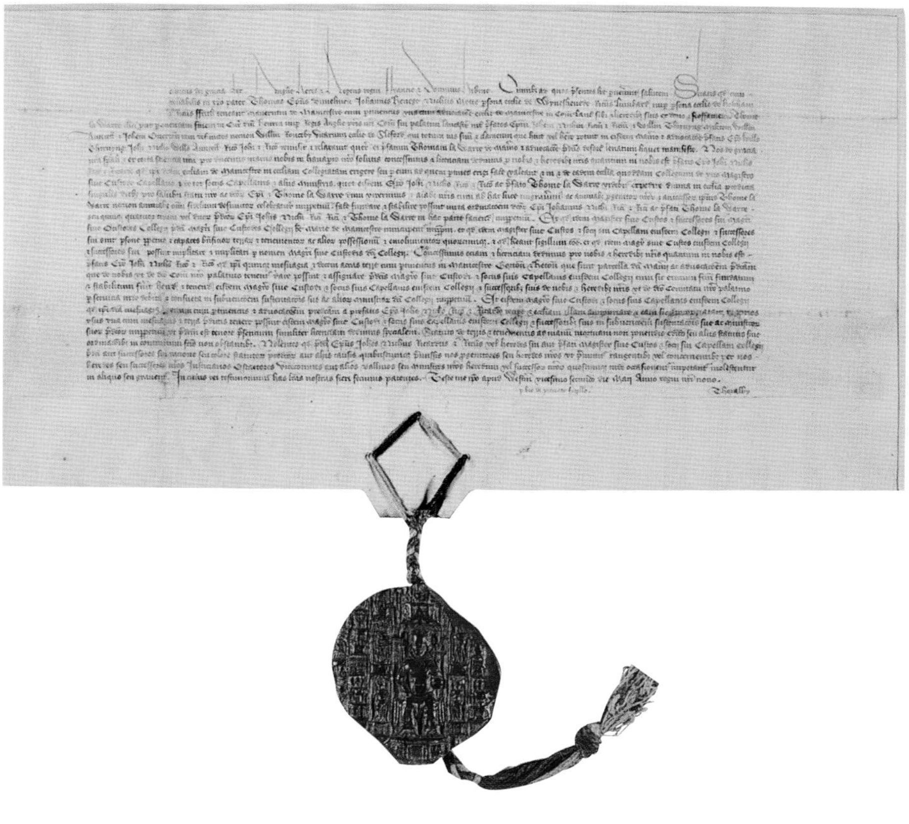

12. The charter of foundation with the seal of Henry V. Reproduced by kind permission of the Dean and Canons of Manchester Cathedral

Overleaf: 13. The warden's lodgings, foreground. The hall range is on the right, the south cloistral range on the left

MINI BUS ONLY

RESERVED
RESERVED

officers and servants as well as regular visitors and guests with their own servants.

Everyday activity for college members would have been governed by the cycle of church life, but they were also part of a domestic community and involved in the running of a large household. They would have eaten together in the hall, with senior members, the priests, or fellows, sitting at a high table at the upper end. The warden may have joined them, though it is possible that he used his own quarters except on special occasions. As with the head of any important household of the day, he had his own private rooms reached from the high end of the hall (Fig. 13). Food was prepared in the huge kitchen under the supervision of the cook, while there was a separate bakery and brew house near the kitchen. Servants brought in food and drink, and cleared up afterwards. We can speculate that high-born men such as the Stanley family members, who were wardens in the late fifteenth century, may have expected a degree of ceremony and observation of a strict hierarchy in the way special meals were conducted. They would have been used to the elaborate household rituals of their close relatives, Lords Stanley and Earls of Derby, and they probably entertained high-ranking family members and other visitors in the college building. The absence of women (all the college servants would have been men) was not unusual. In great medieval households the wives and daughters of the lord and their personal servants were usually the only resident women, forming a very small proportion of the total inhabitants and segregated from many of the day-to-day activities. For example in the 1580s the household of the fourth Earl of Derby consisted of around 115 and 140 people of whom only between three and six were women.[17]

The fellows had rooms with fireplaces they could use for study, and some of their bedrooms were provided with garderobes, or lavatories. The extensive accommodation allowed plenty of room for guests, who may have been given rooms in the gatehouses or elsewhere in the complex. Servants would have lived in, probably in rooms over the bakery and brewhouse. The mention of a 'horsekeper' reminds us that the warden, and perhaps the priests, would have had their own horses. A stable and a number of other buildings, since demolished, were present on the site when a valuation was made *c.* 1654 (*see* p. 87). These included a corn barn, hay barn, a second gatehouse near the church, and a slaughterhouse. It is likely that some or all of these structures related to the college of priests, giving an indication of the original extent of the complex.

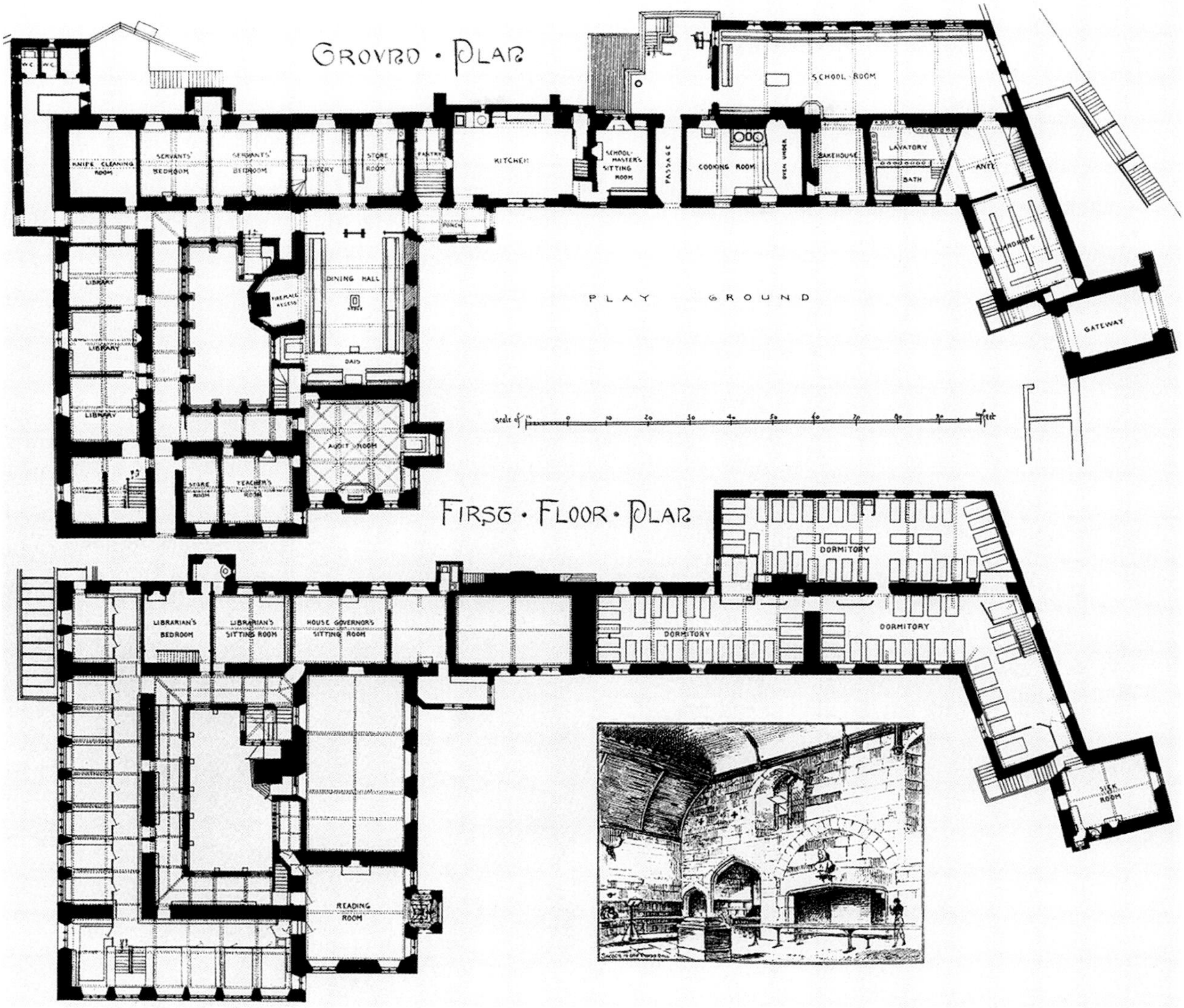

14. Plans of the building prepared by Alfred Waterhouse, *British Architect and Northern Engineer,* 1876

15. The buildings from the courtyard with the central hall flanked by the warden's lodgings, left, and the porch, right. The range on the right incorporates the kitchen and rooms used for baking, brewing and servants' accommodation

THE COLLEGE BUILDING

The old Grelley manor house site was known as Baronshull and Baronsyard, and de la Warre gave this area, conveniently close to the church, to the new foundation. College lands included a narrow strip connecting the premises to the north side of the church.[18] It is not clear what condition the manor house was in, or even if it was standing at that time, but there is no evidence that any part of it was incorporated into the new work. There were ample funds for a new and impressive building, and construction started from scratch using the purple-red sandstone from the nearby Collyhurst quarries, a principal source of stone in Manchester until the nineteenth century. Recent tree-ring analysis, (see Appendix 3), sampled roof and ceiling timbers in the hall and cloister ranges. This showed they were constructed using green (unseasoned) timbers and that

16. The gatehouse shown in an early nineteenth-century drawing by John Palmer. The building on the right is the former Manchester Grammar School. Greater Manchester County Record Office

building was probably underway by 1424 and certainly by 1429. The timbers exhibit similarities in patterns of growth which suggest that they may have all come from the same woodland source.[19]

When complete the premises, shown in plan, Fig. 14, offered generous and comfortable quarters for the nineteen members of the college, their guests and servants. Apart from the church it would almost certainly have been the largest building in the centre of the medieval town, and probably the only other one to be built entirely of stone. The approach is from a narrow thoroughfare off Long Millgate, where an original gatehouse, dwarfed by its neighbours, leads into the site. Here the building and its setting can be appreciated at last. With warm red sandstone walls and stone slate roofs, an L-shaped block fronts its original spacious courtyard (Fig. 15). The large hall, open through two storeys to the roof timbers, has service rooms at the north end, with accommodation above, and two-storey lodgings for the warden at the other end. Out of sight on the west side a three-range two-storey cloister, where other college members had rooms, lies beside the hall around a courtyard. The kitchen is attached to the north-east end of the main building with a range of service accommodation extending eastwards from it. This unorthodox position can probably be explained by the constraints of the site, which falls very steeply down to the river on the north side, and the positioning of the building could have been influenced by access points to the manor house site from the street and the constraints imposed by the inner ditch if it was still open at that time. Medieval rentals and deeds indicate that development along Long Millgate was underway by 1334,[20] and it was probably built-up by the fifteenth century.

The gabled gatehouse (Fig. 16) has a tall archway with huge double doors and a passageway with a flat ceiling with exposed timbers. The blocked door opening on the north side is possibly the one inserted in the seventeenth century to connect with the schoolyard of the then neighbouring Manchester Grammar School.[21] On the courtyard side a flight of external stairs leads to the spacious, heated gatehouse chamber and also gives access to the upper part of the adjacent range. The gatehouse stands on a plinth, unlike the neighbouring part of the building. On the south side a section of the original precinct wall, with obvious signs of rebuilding, extends between former Grammar School buildings fronting Long Millgate and twentieth-century extensions in the courtyard.

Facing the entrance the hall range is the first to be seen, and architectural embellishment is concentrated on this elevation. The ornate windows generally have paired or triple cinquefoil lights with quatrefoils at the intersections under

17. A drawing of *c.* 1815 by John Palmer showing the building before later nineteenth-century alterations. Greater Manchester County Record Office

four-centred arches, most with labels. Elsewhere there are cinquefoiled and trefoiled windows beneath flat heads, some of nineteenth-century origin. Three large transomed windows light the hall, and at the dais (south) end, there is a low two-light window. The whole of this range has a hollow-moulded plinth which is continued around the range attached to the west of the senior lodgings.

The lodgings on the south side of the hall are enriched with a full-height gabled bay with a niche in the gable, and the status of the rooms here is underlined by the elaborate three-light upper window. The south side has arched cinquefoil two-light windows on the east side of a chimney breast, whilst on the other side windows not forming part of the view of the building from the main approach have flat heads. An early nineteenth-century drawing (Fig. 17) shows that before mid-nineteenth-century restoration the gable was enlivened by pinnacles. On the north side of the hall, at the angle with the kitchen, there is a two-storey gabled porch, which was largely rebuilt by the Manchester architect J.E. Gregan during the 1850s. Before that time, as the illustration shows, it had a flat roof and a parapet enriched with quatrefoils instead of the present gable and niche. The porch wall is set back to make room for the adjacent hall window (as it was prior to Gregan's rebuilding). It is not completely clear whether this resulted from alteration necessitated by the remodelling of the hall windows, or if it just a compromise because the porch was secondary, for which there is evidence internally. It is perhaps worth noting that the architect John Palmer, who made a study of the building in around 1815, and Gregan himself, both believed that the porch was a later addition.

Original door openings are generally four-centred or two-centred arches, those in higher status areas usually have continuous hollow mouldings and angle splays, while others are more simply treated. In the porch, doors lead off to the kitchen and cellar, though the stairs were floored over in the late nineteenth century. This wide stone flight of steps can be seen in the extensive cellars which run beneath the service rooms and north cloistral range. Ahead, an archway leads into the screens passage with the expected entrances to buttery and pantry, for storage of food and drink. The eastern room was slightly narrower than its fellow, and the two were thrown together at some point in the late nineteenth century, when a new stair leading down to the cellars was introduced.

The hall (Fig. 18) is a marvellous survival, exceptionally complete and well preserved, with an open timber roof, screen, dais and canopy. At forty-three foot six by twenty-four foot three, it is comparable with the hall at the sixteenth-century Ordsall Hall, Salford (forty-two foot six by twenty-five foot) and not much smaller than the late fifteenth-century Rufford Hall, Lancashire (forty-six foot six by twenty-two foot nine).[22] The seven-foot oak screen is in three sections, the moveable central part now fixed. It is an example of a type favoured in the timber halls of the north west of England, seen in its most elaborate form at Rufford of *c.* 1530. The decorative treatment is relatively simple with moulded rails and some narrow bands of cusped panelling. The embattled cresting is secondary, though it is shown on early nineteenth-century engravings, and could be a restoration. At the other end of the room, where the high table for senior household members was traditionally placed, there is a dais and a coved canopy rising to an embattled tie beam.

A big inglenook fireplace on the west side is a late nineteenth-century rebuilding of one probably inserted in the sixteenth or seventeenth century to replace a central hearth. This can be inferred from the arrangement of roof timbers, where paired principal roof trusses and additional purlins indicate the position of a louvre from which smoke escaped. Plans made before the rebuilding (Fig. 14) show the base of the chimney set at an angle to accommodate the original entrance to the cloister yard at its north-east corner, and the illustration on the plan suggests the fireplace was fairly simply treated with a very shallow arched lintel, quite unlike the huge kitchen fireplace with its flat lintel of joggled stones.

The west wall shows signs of extensive rebuilding necessitated by the insertion of the chimney. The windows on either side of the chimney have obviously been re-set, and vertical joints in the masonry on the north side indicate the dismantling of a whole section of wall, probably when an external staircase was inserted in the seventeenth century. On the south side of the fireplace a square bay is lit by a three-light cinquefoiled window. Above it quatrefoil openings, or squints, are incorporated into the masonry to give views of the hall from a little room above the bay.

The windows on the east side of the hall are also misaligned with the bay divisions of the roof and the feet of the principal roof trusses have all been cut to accommodate the openings, apart from those of the northernmost bay and the one on the west side of the second bay, which rise from foliated stone bosses. This suggests that the present windows are secondary, perhaps enlargements of the original openings, made to improve the lighting of the room. They are similar

in style to other windows of the complex indicating that this was an improvement undertaken at the latest in the late fifteenth or sixteenth century. The awkward junction between window and porch suggests that the introduction of the latter, if it is indeed a later addition, may not have been part of the same phase of alteration.

The handsome roof with deeply moulded timbers and arched braces is an impressive sight, exposed throughout the whole of the building and of uniform design. It is a type of crown-post roof relatively uncommon in English northern and western building traditions, differing in some respects from the usual form and apparently without local parallels (see Appendix 2).

18. The hall looking towards the screens passage

At the south-west corner of the hall a door leads to a lobby with access to the parlour and stairs to the upper chamber and upper south cloister walk. The rooms here must have been the warden's lodgings, though there is a possibility that the fellows used the ground-floor parlour as a common room. The two rooms are the most richly appointed of the complex and both are heated, though the fireplaces and chimneys have been renewed. The fact that the fireplaces do not share the same flue, being in the south and north walls respectively, may indicate that they were put in at different times.

In the lower room, known as the Audit Room, the bay has a stone ceiling with a quatrefoil design. The most notable decorative feature is the timber ceiling (Fig. 19), the only one of its type in the building. On the east and west sides of the room truncated arched braces at the corners support the ceiling timbers. The ceiling is divided into nine panels by moulded ribs decorated with bosses at the intersections, including some with grotesque designs, such as the striking *Mouth of Hell* mask with a sinner trapped in its jaws. In the central panel an eagle grasps a scroll, and though it could be coincidental, the use of an eagle, a badge of the

19. Medieval timber ceiling in the Audit Room. The *Mouth of Hell* mask can be seen top centre

Stanley family, Earls of Derby, may indicate that the ceiling was put in or altered by one of the Stanley wardens during the final quarter of the fifteenth century. There are similarities with the timber roof of the choir of Manchester Cathedral, though this is more elaborate. In both cases each panel is subdivided by slender diagonal ribs with foliated terminations and bosses at the intersections. The flowing foliation of the bosses is similar, and bosses are generally made up of separately carved sections laid one on top of the other. Some of them have similar motifs, in particular those with rose designs. All this is in contrast to the Cathedral nave roof in which bosses are carved from the solid and where there is no intermediate division of panels.

The dating of the Cathedral choir roof presents problems, but it is possible that the decorative details (as opposed to the structural timbers, which may have been earlier but were replaced during nineteenth-century restoration) relate to the alteration of the choir almost certainly undertaken by Warden James Stanley II (incumbent 1485–1506), *c.* 1500, a supposition supported by the presence of Stanley eagles in the roof.[23]

Stone stairs lead up from the lobby outside the hall to a landing where a doorway opens into the south part of the upper cloister walkway. Another doorway at a higher level leads to the upper chamber. The difference in floor level between upper chamber and cloister is around eighteen inches, which suggests that the south cloister range, at least, was not built at the same time as the hall and lodgings. Another explanation would be that the ranges were built sequentially, starting with the north cloister range, followed by that to the west and south, when a gradual loss of level could have occurred during the building work. The cloister doorway has a carved wooden surround with lobed trefoils in the spandrels, fifteenth-century work, though it may not be in its original position. An identical surround survives in the head teacher's apartment above the pantry and buttery. The stone stairs have obviously been renewed or rebuilt, probably in the late nineteenth-century. The windows lighting the stair are seventeenth-century in character, mullioned with flat heads, suggesting alteration or rebuilding at this time as well.

The upper chamber, now the library reading room, is sumptuous (Fig. 20). The bay is the most elaborate and decorative part of the entire building, with a richly moulded stone Tudor arch with clustered shafts rising from tall polygonal bases, and equally rich mouldings between the windows, rising to a stone vaulted ceiling. The windows in the sides of the bay have three lights, of which the innermost are blind on both sides, being within the thickness of the walls. Early views confirm that this is not a result of nineteenth-century restoration. The Stanley badges on the vault appear to be a nineteenth-century addition. Although they are mentioned in an account of 1851,[24] these and similar emblems in the wallplate are not shown in an engraving of 1828[25] or in a drawing of about 1815 by the architect John Palmer (Fig. 21),[26] who was an enthusiastic antiquarian, and would hardly have omitted such an important detail.

The feet of the principal roof trusses were truncated in the seventeenth century, probably to make room for panelling. The one above the bay opening has also been altered, apparently incorporating a new piece of timber and it has been cut, but this would obviously not be necessary for the insertion of panelling. Though it is impossible to know when this was done, this may be an indication that it was modified to accommodate the bay. One would expect a graceful termination to the timber if a bay had been planned from the outset. It is of course possible that there was a pendant which was later removed, but

20. The bay in the warden's lodgings

the alteration to this part of the roof structure is a possible indication that the bay was added, perhaps as part of the campaign which saw refenestration of the hall. The bay appears to be structurally independent, and there is no access to the roof space above the vault. The gabled roof was rebuilt or altered in the mid-nineteenth century, so the original arrangement may be irretrievable.

Three doorways, all with panelled seventeenth-century doors, are ranged along the west side of the room. The first, on the left side, leads into the south cloistral room. Next is the access to the upper cloister walkway and stairs down to the hall. The last leads to a cramped passage with an internal medieval door, giving on to a narrow room with a decorative timber arch on the hall side. It has often been supposed that this originated as a gallery overlooking the hall which

21. Drawing of *c.* 1815 by John Palmer showing the bay. Greater Manchester County Record Office

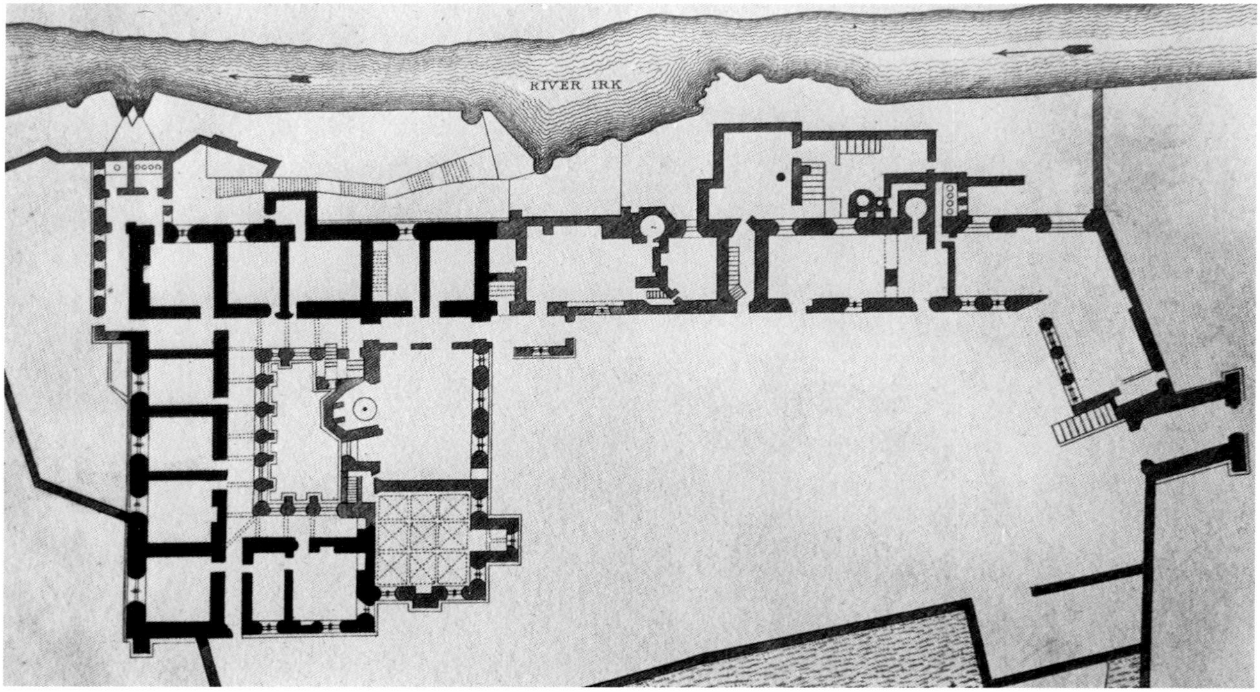

22. Plan of the ground floor of the building by John Palmer, 1815

was subsequently walled up, but strangely the timber arch is not finished on the inner side, suggesting that it was not in fact meant to be seen from the hall. This is a very puzzling feature and it is difficult to be certain of the original arrangement. The row of sawn-off tenons in the rafters on the courtyard side is also difficult to explain. Squints in the stonework give views into the hall, and on the outer wall there is a row of nine mullioned windows with cusped arched heads. Iron brackets for shutters suggest that they were not originally glazed. If not originally a gallery, what could this little room have been used for? It looks as if it must have been exclusively for the use of the warden, but whether he used it as a store, oratory or for some other purpose, we can only speculate.

THE CLOISTER

Rooms for the fellows, known as sets as they are in Oxford and Cambridge colleges, were in the three cloister ranges around a courtyard on the west side of the hall, approached by cloister walkways on two levels. A plan of 1815 (Fig. 22) shows the arrangement before later nineteenth-century alterations.

The cloister courtyard is one of the most atmospheric spaces in the building (Fig. 23). A mutilated window at the south-west corner forms the entrance, leading into the little yard paved with natural river cobbles, with a restored well

23. The cloister courtyard

24. Cloister buttress resting on the plinth of the hall range

head near the centre. The projecting and receding walls and buttresses, the elaborate plinth and the sense of enclosure, lend a sense of intimacy and make the cloister seem less monumental than the rest of the building. Stepped buttresses divide the bays, and the one at the south-east corner sits unhappily atop the hall plinth, showing that this side of the cloister walkway postdates the hall range (Fig. 24). The difference in level between the senior lodgings and south cloister has already been noted. The hall plinth is lower and more simply treated than that of the cloister, which is stepped and integrated with the window sills. Windows of a design unique to this part of the building light the lower walkway. Three cinquefoil lights are divided by mullions reaching to the top of the opening instead of intersecting. These windows may originally have been unglazed, and the remains of two seventeenth-century shutters which fit the openings exactly are preserved in the building (see Appendix 3), suggesting that glazing may have been introduced, possibly for the first time, after that date. Upper windows light alternate bays only. They are of similar design to those in the hall and lodgings, having two lights with trefoil heads, though the quatrefoils are blind.

25. The west cloister walkway

The lower cloister walkway (Fig. 25) has a ceiling with moulded camber beams and there are signs that the south corridor has been partitioned off at some time.

Corridors extend from the walkways, leading on the north side to a small garden and covered access (added in the seventeenth century) to steps formerly leading down to the River Irk. The west cloister walkway leads to the main courtyard. The camber-beam roof is not continued in the corridors, making a clear distinction in the hierarchy of space. The single and paired entrances to the sets from the cloister walkway on the ground floor are of the type used for the buttery and pantry entrances, that is two-centred arches with continuous hollow moulding and angle splays, though the entrance in the north corridor lacks these enrichments. Room partitions are timber-framed where they survive, except those at the north-west and south-west corners. The north and south ranges of the sets have outer walls of stone, with the west range slotted between them, possibly indicating phased building campaigns.

All the partitions between the upper rooms were removed for construction of the library, but the bay divisions of the roof correspond with the original room divisions. Although the upper rooms have now been thrown into one space, the cloister walkway and original entrances from it have survived, though the walkway ceiling has been replaced. Access to the upper cloister walk was via a stairway in the northern corridor, where the partition to the set on the south side is recessed from the line of the passageway, making it the smallest of all the apartments. Timbers relating to this stair can be seen in the ceiling. The entrances to the upper rooms are like those below, except that they lack the hollow moulding. With the exception of the south range, upper and lower entrances are superimposed.

Each set consists of two rooms, one on top of the other, reached respectively from the upper and lower cloister walkways. The accommodation is unusually generous, as it seems probable that each of the fellows had exclusive use of one set. Although this is no match for the individual vicars' houses at Wells (*c.* 1357, possibly rebuilt in the fifteenth century) or Windsor (1478–81), lodgings of this type were more usually shared, for example in the medieval Oxford and Cambridge colleges where, as W.A. Pantin makes clear, 'no-one except the head of a college or a wealthy and dignified lodger expected to have a room to himself'.[27] The lower rooms, which have fireplaces, would probably have been studies, with unheated bedrooms above (see Appendix 1). Altogether there are seven sets of this type, and in addition the suite of rooms over the pantry and buttery which connects with a room in the upper part of the porch. These interconnecting rooms are reached from the north-west end of the cloister, and are provided with a garderobe. The eight fellows could have been comfortably accommodated in these rooms, while rooms for the clerks and choristers were probably in the upper range of the east kitchen wing.

Windows lighting the upper and lower rooms of the sets were almost all replaced, those in the upper rooms when the Chetham's library was created in the seventeenth century, and those in the lower rooms in the nineteenth century. The head of one original window can be seen in the masonry in the inner face of the south-west library wall, while some of the windows on the north side facing the Irk and on the south side at ground floor level seem to have retained the original form, with paired lights and cusped heads.

Two sets of the northern range share a double garderobe, or lavatory, but if any of the other cloistral rooms had this facility later alterations have removed any traces of them. Perhaps garderobes were provided only on the north side of the building which allowed easy drainage into the river.

The rooms off the south side of the cloister are arranged differently from their counterparts on other sides. Doorways from the warden's lodgings lead directly into them on both upper and lower levels, and if this was the original arrangement they must either have been part of the senior lodgings, or they may

26. The north and west sides of the building, by John Palmer, *c.* 1815. The main kitchen chimney is shown at the centre of the north range (left side). On the other side the windows of the library, inserted in the seventeenth century, can be seen. The bridge over the River Irk is on the right in the foreground. Greater Manchester County Record Office

have had a special function. There is a possibility that the upper room could have been a chapel. Interestingly, this part of the library is called the Mary Chapel, though it is not known when the usage originated.

On the ground floor the two rooms are of unequal size, a large room entered from a doorway in the south cloister walkway, and a much smaller room with a later doorway. Original access to the little room was probably via a connecting door between the two rooms, as shown on the 1815 plan (Fig. 22). The larger room has an entrance from the south cloister walk distinguished from all the others of the cloister by the presence of a hood mould (Fig. 47), possibly an indication that it was originally exposed to the weather, and that the cloister walkway here is secondary. The room was connected to the ground floor part of the warden's lodgings by an arched doorway which is concealed by seventeenth-century panelling in that room, but visible on the other side and shown as a recess on plan. The opening has been plastered over so it is difficult to suggest a date for it.

On the upper level there is no entrance from the south cloister walkway, only a doorway from the upper part of the warden's lodgings. There is no sign of an internal stair, and the medieval ceiling is intact, showing that there was no internal access from the lower floor. This suggests either that the room could only be entered from the warden's lodgings or that the whole of the upper south range was one long room, reached from the upper entrance to the south-west set. There are other anomalies in the upper floor arrangements, for example a slight setback of the north wall at the west end, where the roof has a slightly different pitch. The presence of a boss in the roof here is also without parallels elsewhere in the building. It is of identical design to examples found in the nave roof of Manchester Cathedral and also in Eccles Parish church, in nearby Salford, in which four praying figures surmount a sun-in-splendour motif. Unfortunately the dates of both these other examples have not been satisfactorily established, though the sun-in-splendour is a badge of the York family and may indicate a date before 1485. The Cathedral nave is anecdotally attributed to Warden Langley (incumbent 1465–81), which would fit with this theory, and if this is so we can speculate that Langley may have been responsible for adding the boss and perhaps making other alterations, though the possibility that it was brought from elsewhere at a later date should not be discounted.

Other inconsistencies in the south cloister range include the fact that the doorway from the warden's parlour to the cloister is not aligned with the walkway, while the fact that the whole range projects forward of the line of the senior lodgings is another indication that it was a later addition or resulted from changes of plan or faulty setting-out during the construction of the building.

27. The kitchen interior

Endowments

KITCHEN AND EAST WING

The kitchen has an attached range to the east which provided rooms for brewing and baking, with quarters for servants and other household members. Some impression of the dramatic appearance of this and the remaining north side of the building is given by views made before the Irk was culverted, when it had a positively fortress-like appearance with sheer walls rising up from the riverside (Fig. 26). The large arched opening below cellar level in this view is one of two (now invisible), which may have been boat houses. The whole of the east range is distinguished from other parts of the complex by its double string course and the absence of a plinth, though if this indicates a separate building campaign the fact that it has exactly the same roof structure as the main range suggests that not much time can have elapsed between building phases.

The kitchen is almost as impressive as the hall, open through two storeys and furnished with huge fireplaces (Fig. 27). It is lit from the south side by three pairs of upper windows with cinquefoil heads, the westernmost light blocked by the porch but visible inside, a result of the 1850s rebuild. A rebate at sill level continues the line almost to the west wall, suggesting that there may originally have been another pair of windows, forming a continuous range along the wall. If this was the case, symmetry would be restored to the upper openings here, and this would be a clear indication that the windows must have been blocked when the porch was built.

A wide slightly recessed arch in the south wall is a puzzling feature for which an explanation is difficult to devise, though the suggestion that there was originally a fireplace in this position should not perhaps, be ruled out. There is no evidence for the presence of a central hearth in the arrangement of roof timbers, so the fireplaces may be primary. That in the north wall has a joggled lintel, with a tall relieving arch over, and there is a similar, smaller fireplace in the east wall. Various recesses beside the fireplaces would presumably have been used as larders and stores. The small blocked opening high in the west wall must have been a spy hole, giving sight of the kitchen from the rooms above the pantry and buttery, probably added in the seventeenth century, like the one in the hall. Henry Taylor, writing in 1884, saw it before it was blocked up, when it was furnished with iron bars.[28] The north chimney was rebuilt in 1903–4 and that to the east was decommissioned and altered when stairs leading down to cellars and up to the upper part of the east range were inserted. This work was probably undertaken in the later nineteenth century, as Waterhouse shows the stairs in his 1876 plans (Fig. 14) but Palmer, in 1815, does not (Fig. 22). A narrow passageway leads to the neighbouring room which has a corner oven.

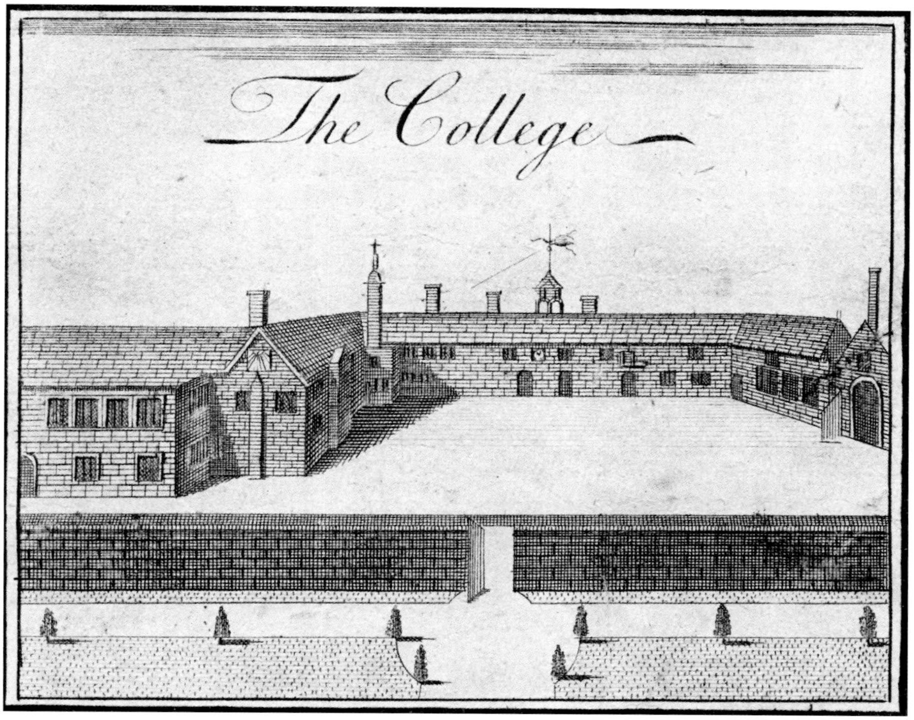

28. The earliest known detailed view of the building from Casson & Berry's map of Manchester, published in 1741

The kitchen and adjoining room are separated from the other accommodation at ground floor level by a passageway leading from the main courtyard to a smaller courtyard on the north side of the building which is sited on an elevated stone platform, and where an extension of 1844 now occupies part of the space. This passageway once contained a stairway, though the only visible evidence for it now is in the set-back of the west wall and the stair window in the north elevation above the passageway. The stair is shown on the 1815 plan (Fig. 22) and it was supplanted at some time during the nineteenth century by the one in the kitchen chimney. It gave access to two upper rooms, and if this was the original fifteenth-century arrangement, they could be candidates for the clerks' accommodation, 'chumming' together two to a room.

A polygonal timber bellcote rises from the roof of the room beside the passageway. It has a lead roof and arcaded openings with pendants, as shown on an engraving of 1741 (Fig. 28). The roof timbers were replaced or heavily modified when it was introduced, perhaps in the early eighteenth century. The principals rise from classical brackets and the supporting structure straddles the main roof timbers.

Ground-floor rooms east of the passageway retain some early features, though both seventeenth-century and later alterations make the original arrangements difficult to retrieve. In particular the openings and probably whole sections of

29. The roof timbers in the angled service range between the gatehouse and kitchen

the south wall in the short angled range beside the gatehouse and the immediately adjacent bays appear to have been altered or rebuilt in the seventeenth century and remodelled in medieval style in the mid-nineteenth century (see Appendix 4). A porter's room with a narrow slit window lies at the south end beside the gatehouse. The upper apartments have widely spaced roof trusses suggesting the presence of large undivided spaces, and the way in which the timbers are contrived to take the corner at the angle of this section is a very impressive sight (Fig. 29).

In reviewing the architectural evidence, it is clear that a number of changes were made to the building after it went up in the 1420s, though some of the anomalies might be the result of changes of plan or miscalculation during the initial building phase. Other alterations and improvements might have been made decades later. Evidence that work was undertaken by Warden Langley and one or both of the Stanley wardens is certainly slight, but the character of secondary work points to a date no later than the sixteenth century. It may even be that some alterations were made by the Earls of Derby, though the college was never a principal residence of the family. It is also possible that there was a more thorough-ranging programme of alteration and additions than has been suggested. For example the hall bay and perhaps the stairs to the upper warden's room, with the gallery over, are all parts of the building which could have been added or enlarged. It is even possible that part of the outer walls of the building were originally timber-framed, and were later rebuilt in stone, though the close conformity between the roof structure and arrangement of internal spaces makes it seem unlikely that there could have been wholesale rebuilding. These points notwithstanding, the most astonishing fact about the building is that the degree of change after the sixteenth century was so limited, and that on the whole the later alterations are easy to disentangle from earlier building phases.

CHAPTER TWO

Domine Dilexi Decorum Domus Tuae[29]

The Wardens of the College and the Collegiate Church

The college's founder, Thomas de la Warre, did not live to see completion of the building, but the first warden, John Huntingdon (d. 1458) carried forward the work after de la Warre's death in 1426.[30] Before being recruited by de la Warre, Huntingdon had been rector of St Michael's Church, Ashton-under-Lyne, where rebuilding had started *c.* 1413. During his incumbency as warden he began work on rebuilding the chancel at Manchester, and although this was probably not completed in his lifetime, it seems certain that the college buildings, or at least the main hall and cloister range, had been completed by the time he died in 1458. Huntingdon's restored brass can be seen in the choir of the Cathedral (Fig. 31)

30. Seal of the College depicting the Assumption of the Virgin with shields of the Grelley and de la Warre families, Lords of the Manor. It is attached to a licence of Warden James Stanley II for worship in the newly founded Jesus Chapel, 1506. The document is in the Chetham's Library collection, and the seal is the only surviving example of a seal of the Manchester College

31. The brass of warden John Huntingdon in Manchester Cathedral. Reproduced by kind permission of the Dean and Canons of Manchester Cathedral

and his rebus, a punning pictorial device expressing his name, appears high up at the west end of the choir roof, though it is difficult to see except on the brightest of days. A carving on one side shows a hunting scene with a man and dogs, and on the other side the man draws ale from a barrel, or tun, making up the word 'huntingtun'. The scenes are reprised in a nineteenth-century carving at the entrance to the Lady Chapel and a similar device was recorded in the stalls of Ashton-under-Lyne church, before destruction in the eighteenth century.

Chetham's Library has some of Huntingdon's papers, including his will. This is dated 1454 and leaves money for 'edificacion, expences, costes, and bygging [building] of the newe work begonen [begun] by me in the Chauncell', making it sound as if the work was not finished when he made the will, and perhaps not even at the time of his death four years later. His brass memorial in the Cathedral choir also records the building work, though the restorers had to rely on a transcription of 1650 to reconstruct the wording, which includes the phrase 'Qui de novo construxit istam Cancellam' [who built this chancel anew]. A label above the figure has a line from Psalm 26, usually translated: 'Lord I have loved the habitation of thy house'.

Although relatively little is known about Huntingdon's incumbency, the record suddenly comes to life with a description of events that appear in an undated petition of complaint made by Huntingdon to the King.[31] Forty people, members of the Booth family and their associates, had entered the church forcibly during compline to try to seize one of the fellows of the college, Thomas Barbour, against whom they had an unspecified grievance. Barbour managed to escape and fled to the college. Undeterred, the Booths called upon their allies, including John Byron, William Lever and William Massey of Worsley, who allegedly assembled a company of five hundred armed men, such a large number that it is tempting to think that Huntingdon may have been exaggerating. The college was besieged and its members threatened with death if they helped Barbour to escape. The warden, fellows and clerks dared not leave the building to celebrate church services, and the King was petitioned to resolve the situation. Unfortunately we do not know what Barbour was accused of, nor anything more about this intriguing event and how it was resolved.

The second warden, Roger Radclyffe, was a member of the branch of the family occupying Radcliffe Tower, which survives as a ruin in Radcliffe, near Bury. He was followed in 1465 by Ralph Langley, one of the Langleys of Agecroft, who had been the rector of Prestwich church. He is credited with making 'the Clocke and Chime in Manchester Church with his owne handes' as well as rebuilding the nave of the church, though no contemporary documentary evidence has been identified which would support this.[32] The fourth warden was James Stanley, youngest son of the first Lord Stanley, Sir Thomas. On his death

in 1485, after only four years in the post, he was succeeded by James Stanley II (d. 1515), the youngest son of Thomas, second Lord Stanley and first Earl of Derby, by his first wife.

James Stanley II was wealthy and well connected. His father's second wife was Lady Margaret Beaufort, mother of Henry VII, an alliance which consolidated the family's influence in the highest court circles. Lady Margaret was a patron of architecture and learning and noted for her piety.[33] Several members of her household had strong Manchester connections and some were members of the college. One of the best-known was Hugh Oldham, the founder of Manchester Grammar School, who was her receiver and chancellor, and went on to become Bishop of Exeter. She has been credited with personal involvement with some of her stepson's building campaigns at the collegiate church, which included co-sponsorship of the magnificent choir furnishings, installed *c.* 1500–6 (Fig. 32), and the building of the St John the Baptist or Derby Chapel (now the Regimental Chapel), probably after 1513. The stalls in the choir, designed for use by members of the college and now used by the Dean and Canons of the cathedral, are remarkably fine. They were carved either by the workshop of William Bromflet

32. The choir stalls in Manchester Cathedral looking west. Reproduced by kind permission of the Dean and Canons of Manchester Cathedral

or by craftsmen familiar with Bromflet's stalls in Ripon Minster and Beverley Minster.[34] There are thirty places, surmounted by canopies of breathtaking beauty and intricacy. The tip-up seats, or misericords, are carved with a variety of entertaining scenes, including apes robbing a pedlar, a pig playing bagpipes and men playing backgammon (Fig. 33).

Stalls with Stanley emblems and badges abound on the south side, including charming representations of the Lathom legend, in which scenes of an eagle with a child in its nest illustrate a family story concerning a semi-mythical ancestor who was rescued from the eagle's nest and adopted. The Stanleys acquired many of their lands through marriage to the Lathoms in the fourteenth century, and Lathom House in Lancashire was one of their two principal seats.

The architectural evidence suggests that Stanley remodelled the choir, probably to align it with Langley's nave, either re-using or replacing Huntingdon's work, resulting in a splayed plan, narrower at the east than at the west end. The nave may also have been altered at this time, possibly with the insertion of the present clerestory. There are parallels with the work of the East Anglian workshop of the mason John Wastell, who went on to build King's College Chapel in Cambridge. Churches altered or rebuilt by the Stanley family in North Wales also offer some comparisons, suggesting that the family used the same masons for these projects. The work of both masons and woodcarvers is of national standard, using teams from far afield rather than local artisans, a reflection of the standing and aspirations of the Stanley family and the college. Notable furnishings include the superb angel minstrels in the nave roof, though it is not certain whether Stanley or an earlier warden was responsible for these.

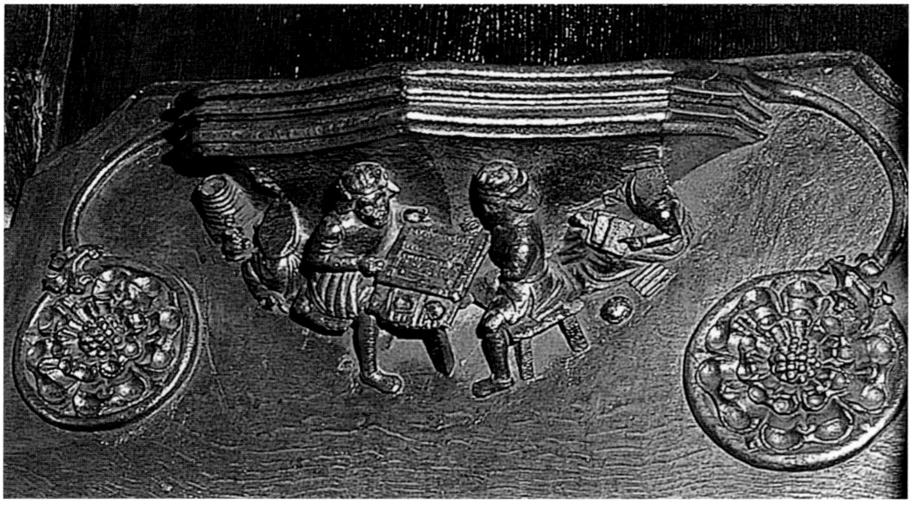

33. Misericord in the choir of Manchester Cathedral showing two men playing backgammon. Reproduced by kind permission of the Dean and Canons of Manchester Cathedral

It is tempting to suggest that alterations to the college buildings might also have been Stanley's work, with the addition of the porch, the insertion or enlargement of the large and ornate hall windows, and perhaps the addition of the bay on the warden's lodgings, which would have given the buildings a grander appearance. Stanley went on to become Bishop of Ely in 1506, and later seems to have been charged with raising an army and putting it into array for the battle of Flodden, where his illegitimate son or grandson John Stanley distinguished himself. He started building the St John the Baptist chapel, now the Regimental Chapel, on the north-east side of the cathedral, possibly in thanksgiving for the victory at Flodden. It is thought to have been finished by John Stanley, and James was buried in a smaller chapel attached at the north-east corner. This was destroyed during the Second World War, but his brass is preserved in the chapel. It shows him in episcopal robes, giving no hint of his rather colourful career. He was described in a sixteenth-century metrical history of the Stanley family as:

> 'A goodly tall man as was in all England
> And spedd well all matters that he took in hand'[35]

When his tomb was opened in 1812 the bones of an unusually tall man were discovered. Other sources show that he organised the first recorded cockfight in Lancashire,[36] and lapses from celibacy which resulted in at least one illegitimate child led one commentator to describe him as 'more voluptuous than virtuous'.[37]

Stanley almost certainly secured the warden's post for Robert Cliff, his successor, and it seems that the family chaplain, Richard Alday, was presented but never confirmed as warden thereafter. George West, a descendant of the College's founder, followed, but later resigned, and George Collier was the last warden to occupy the position before dissolution. Recent research suggests that Collier, later aided by Warden Laurence Vaux, was involved in trying to save some of the church treasures, including vestments and plate. These were deposited at Standish Hall, near Wigan and at a monastery in Belgium. Vaux's will makes it clear that the intention was to preserve them until the old faith was restored. Part of one of the vestments, thought to date from the late fourteenth century, has recently been identified. It is an exquisite example of embroidery showing the Assumption of the Virgin, a scene of the pregnant virgin with St Elizabeth, and a number of figures who were probably donors.[38]

A TRVE AND FVLL RELATION, OF THE TROVBLES IN *LANCASHIERE*;

between the Lord *Strange*, now Earle of *Derby*; And the well-affected People of that Countie: with their Valiant Resistance, and full Resolution.

ALSO,

Certain passages between the Earl of *New-Castle*, and Captaine *Hotham* in *York-sheire*.

Sent to a Reverend Divine in LONDON.

LONDON,

Printed for *Edward Blackmoore*, *December* the 9th. 1642

CHAPTER THREE

'The Earl of Derbie's House in Manchester'

The Reformation and After

The college was dissolved in 1547 under the second Chantries Act, which continued the dismantling of ecclesiastical institutions started by Henry VIII with the Dissolution of the Monasteries in 1536. Little had been done to put the first Chantries Act into effect and the second Act, which provided for the confiscation and dissolution of the chantries, was implemented by Edward VI, who came to the throne in 1547. A buyer was quickly found for the Manchester College, in the shape of Edward Stanley, third Earl of Derby. The 1549 *Grant by letters patent of Edward VI of the College House to Edward, third Earl*

34. Title page of an account by Thomas Jesland of the siege of Manchester during the Civil War in 1642

35. Grant by letters patent of Edward VI transferring ownership of the college to the third Earl of Derby, dated 9 July 1549

36. Warden John Dee from a drawing in the Chetham's Library collection

of Derby[39] is preserved in Chetham's Library (Fig. 35). Derby had purchased a number of monastic and chantry estates in the years following the Dissolution, usually choosing property close to his existing holdings. This included the Dieulacres estate in Staffordshire and land formerly belonging to Burscough Priory, for which the family held the lay patronage, in Lancashire and Cheshire. The acquisition of the Manchester property, which included lands given for support of the college, would have been a useful addition to his Lancashire holdings with the bonus of providing a prestigious building in the centre of town.

In 1553 the college was refounded by Queen Mary, and George Collier was reinstated as warden. Elizabeth I dissolved it and refounded it in 1578 under the name Christ's College, when the numbers were reduced. A modified charter was granted by Charles I, in response to lobbying by Humphrey Chetham and his associates, which was aimed at curbing abuses of the wardens. The institution continued until 1847 when the warden and fellows became Dean and Canons of

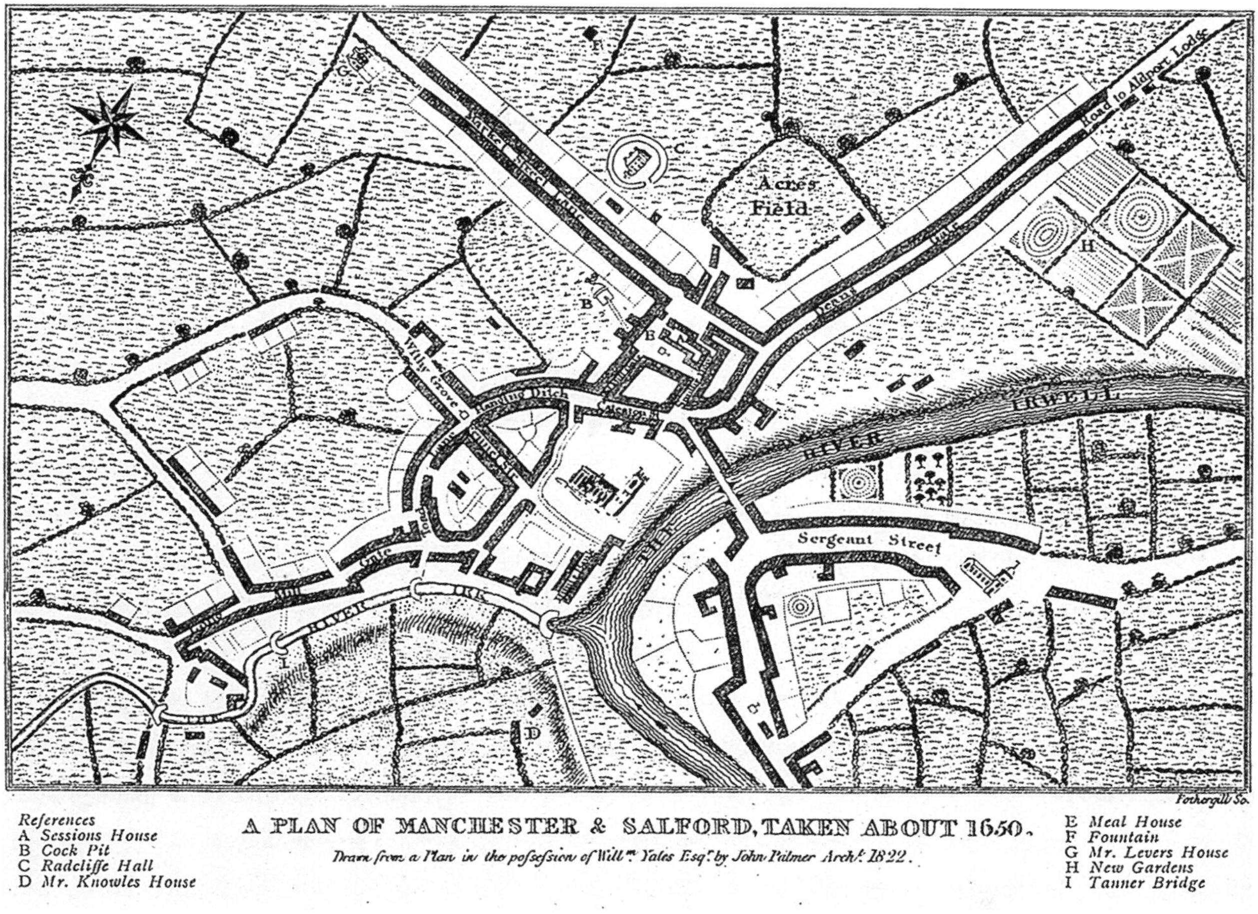

37. Map of Manchester *c.* 1650 showing the extent of the town at the time of the Civil War. The route to Aldport Lodge is indicated top right. The map is orientated with south at the top

the newly created Manchester Cathedral. The actual college building, however, was never restored to the institution, and it was to remain in Stanley hands for almost a century after dissolution. According to the Manchester annalist Richard Hollingworth, it was 'accounted the Earl of Derbie's house in Manchester' and the family were 'careful as our fathers have told us, to provide very well for three or foure ministers officiating in the church'.[40]

It is not known how the Derby family used the buildings. They doubtless had a variety of business and social reasons for visiting the town but they stayed at another property, Aldport Lodge, in Castlefield, on some occasions. It has sometimes been thought that the buildings continued to be used as a residence by the warden and fellows under an arrangement with the family, but this has been substantiated only in the case of John Dee (1527–1608), who seems to have been allowed to live in the buildings as a favour. The valor of the sixth Earl lists the college under the heading 'Estates mortgaged or let on redeemable leases' in 1600, though no income from the property is recorded.[41]

Dee was a brilliant mathematician and geographer who lectured in England and Europe and was offered professorships in Paris and Oxford (Fig. 36). He deserves to be remembered for this and his pioneering lectures on Euclid given in Paris, but he was better known in his day, and our own, for his reputation as a sorcerer earned through chemical experiments and use of a crystal globe and 'magic' stones to try to communicate with spirits and angels. Imprisoned on suspicion of threatening Queen Mary's life by poison or magic, he was later released and subsequently went into the service of Queen Elizabeth I, to whom he acted as astrologer as well as advising on a range of other matters including proposed changes to the calendar. He was given the wardenship of the Manchester college late in his life, and moved there in 1595/6, bringing with him his wife, servants and large family of young children. His time at Manchester was not a happy one. He was an old man and so short of money that he was forced to pawn some of his possessions, including various items of plate which were used as security for a loan from Edward Chetham, High Master of Manchester Grammar School and brother of the hospital founder Humphrey Chetham.

Dee fell out with other members of the college and became embroiled in various arguments and disputes concerning tithes and land holdings. He had unsuccessfully tried to shake off his reputation as a sorcerer, but was nevertheless called upon to exorcise demons from a woman and some children in the Manchester area, which he refused to do. Despite his reputation, or perhaps because of it, he received a variety of visitors. The Earl and Countess of Derby arrived unexpectedly with a party of others including the Earl of Sefton and Sir Richard Molyneux, in June 1596, when they 'cam suddenly upon [me] after 3 of the clok' and had to make do with a 'scholers collation'.[42] The following year the Earl and Countess, who were staying at their house, Aldport Lodge in Castlefield, had 'a banket [meal] at my lodging at the colledg hora _ 4.'[43] Other notable visitors included William Camden, for whom Dee transcribed some Roman inscriptions, and Christopher Saxton the cartographer, who sought his advice on parish boundaries. His diary records various other visitors, to whom he often lent books from his extensive library.

In 1603 the lord of the Manchester manor Nicholas Mosley and others wrote to Sir Robert Cecil, one of Queen Elizabeth I's closest advisers, to complain about Dee, saying: 'Mr Dee the warden, now theire, being noe preacher and not any of the Fellowes but one comorant [resident] within the said towne, there is no such constant and acceptable course of ministerie houlden there as her Majestie entended by the Foundacon'.[44] The letter was aimed at persuading the Queen to dismiss Dee and instate William Bourne in his place. Dee left Manchester the following year, but he remained warden of the college in his absence until his death in 1608. Some of his books, with his own annotations and marginal notes, are now in Chetham's library, including one by Konrad Gesner published in 1555 on medical, chemical and pharmacological subjects, which bears the signature of John Barker of Hopwood, near Middleton, Rochdale, suggesting that he may have lent or sold it while living in Manchester. His 1567 edition of Vitruvius was acquired by the architect John Soane in 1805 before finding its way into the Chetham's collection.

There is some evidence for repair or alteration to the building around the time of Dee's residency. Tree-ring analysis has shown that some timbers on the north side of the cloistral range date from the late sixteenth or early seventeenth centuries, and are similar to undateable timbers on the west side of the hall. This work could possibly have been associated with the insertion of the chimney. This is the only evidence for post-Reformation Stanley intervention into the fabric of the building. The family could have had improvements or repairs done in anticipation of Dee arriving, or perhaps after he left. They sold Aldport Lodge in 1599, and may have expected to use the college buildings themselves during subsequent visits to Manchester.

THE CIVIL WAR AND AFTER

The fortunes of the Stanley family suffered a serious setback during the Civil War, when James, Lord Strange (Fig. 38), who became the seventh Earl of Derby in September 1642, was a principal supporter of Charles I. Although there is evidence that he initially tried to maintain unity between factions in the North

38. James, seventh Earl of Derby. Engraving from *The Stanley Papers,* Chetham Society, 1867

39. The Dowager Countess Charlotte. Engraving from *The Stanley Papers,* Chetham Society, 1867

West of England and to prevent the breakdown of law and order, he went on to play a leading part in the Royalist cause in Lancashire. He led Royalist forces in a siege of Manchester in September 1642, but they were repelled and the town subsequently became a Parliamentary stronghold. The success of resistance in Manchester has been attributed largely to the strategy of Colonel Rosworm, a German soldier and engineer who organised fortifications and defences. The church and churchyard were used as a strategic position in the siege, facing Royalist incursions from across the river in Salford, and Rosworm himself superintended the defence of this position.[45] The college buildings were commandeered, and contemporary accounts describe gunpowder being made there when 'accidentally by the snuff of a Candle falling into some, as it was a making, it blew of some slate of the Colledge and terrified the workmen.'[46] Things were hardly improved by the use of part of the building as a prison, and it is surprising that it did not suffer greater damage.

Stanley influence in the North West of England was effectively curtailed after the siege of their seat, Lathom House, in 1644, and the Royalist defeat at Marston Moor in the same year. From 1643 onwards the Parliamentary Committee for Sequestrations (known from 1644 as the Committee for Compounding with Delinquents) began to take over the Stanley estates. Attempts at negotiation, in which the Earl's fine was fixed at a little over £15,500, came to nothing, and he was never allowed to compound his estates. He was captured and executed in Bolton in 1651. His estates were confiscated and Parliament started to sell them off in the same year, though the college formed part of the jointure of Charlotte, the dowager Countess of Derby (Fig. 39), who was permitted to pay a fine for the recovery of her estates in 1653.[47]

Humphrey Chetham had shown interest in the college buildings before the end of the 1640s. He wanted to use them for a charitable project he had been developing over a number of years, which eventually crystallised as proposals for a charity school, or hospital, for poor boys from the Manchester area, and a public library. Chetham was a well-known and well-connected Manchester merchant, banker and landowner[48] who has been described as 'the most successful gentleman merchant in Caroline Lancashire'.[49] He was born in Crumpsall, north Manchester, into a merchant family. He made his fortune in the cloth trade and acted as a banker to local gentry families, as well as investing in property. Despite his reluctance to accept such posts, he served in a number of official positions including a period as High Sheriff of Lancashire. The fact that he managed to steer a path between the warring political factions of the day and emerge with his fortune and his reputation intact shows that he had well-developed diplomatic skills as well as business acumen. His portrait (Fig. 40), by an unknown artist, shows him wearing an embroidered cap and a ruff,

40. Portrait of Humphrey Chetham by an anonymous artist

holding a pair of gloves. He has a thin face and a beaky nose, and the look from his rather sunken eyes is contemplative, even wary. It is tempting to read into this face some clue to his character. No-one who had lived through the years of uncertainty, turbulence and bloodshed of the Civil War could fail to be affected, and anyone holding public office was particularly vulnerable. Here is a man who had made a fortune, yet there is a look of austerity and seriousness, fitting perhaps for one who intended to give a substantial part of that fortune to charity. It would be easy to read too much into the picture, especially since, as recent research has shown, the first documented reference to it occurs in 1698,

41. The college building after the Civil War as portrayed in the early twentieth century. Recent research suggests the damage was not as extensive as the artist, J.J. Phelps, imagined

and it may have been painted after his death.[50] What is certain however, is that had it not been for his charity, Chetham may have been remembered, if at all, as a hard-headed businessman, who could be as ruthless as he was astute. It was these very attributes, as well as his experience as a trustee of several local charities, which helped him to set up his charity and endow it in a way which ensured its survival.

Towards the end of his life, Chetham, who was unmarried with no children of his own, began to maintain a number of poor boys from the Manchester area, lodging them with respectable families and paying for their upkeep and education. The college building offered an ideal opportunity for placing these arrangements on a more secure footing by establishing a hospital, and Chetham decided to approach the Earl about it. He wrote to Derby's agent to express his interest in March 1648/9 saying:

> . . . I am purposeing & . . . am resolved to make an hospitall at Manchester & for that purpose have thought the Colledge a fitt place & considering the uselesnes of it to his Lordship in the times of Peace, much more so now being sequestered & a great parte of it spoyld & ruind & become like a dunghill as (it may bee) you know, soe that it will never bee fitt for his Lordships use, without as much cost in repairing it, as would build a commodious howse. Its like his Lordship may bee inclind not onely

> to the present using of it for such a purpose, but also the absolute sale thereof hereafter upon reasonable tearmes, when his estate shall come into his owne possession. I doubt not but I could have it of the Sequestrators, but without his honours consent and appro-bacion I shall never make such a mocion . . .[51]

An appended sheet gives a description of the building, used as the basis for a reconstruction of how it may have appeared at that time (Fig. 41). The fact that Chetham was trying to acquire the property at the time may have been reason for casting its condition in the worst possible light:

> yt hath beene a prison a long tyme For as many prisoners as yt would hould and thereby is become most noysome & Fylthy & by making of gun pouther some of the roof is blown of & other stone is Falne of soe as thereby yt is become uninhabitable & the timbers being rotted for [lack] of slate will require great cost to make them usefull the walls that made yt Severall are taken away to make Centeries att divers streets of the towne for as yt lyes comon & the towne swyne make there abode bothe in the yards & house.[52]

Although it is not clear what Lord Derby thought of the proposal, it was in any case necessary to come to terms with the Committee for Compounding with Delinquents. Their attitude was initially favourable, and an agreement was signed in September 1649, but one of the other committee members, Colonel Thomas Birch, later insisted on attaching conditions. Remarks appended to this paper, describing the conditions as a 'sawcie proposal'[53] indicate that Chetham was offended by Birch's imputations – which amounted to an expression of distrust in Chetham's aims – and the disagreement led to abandonment of the scheme.

Birch's opposition to the sale may have been motivated by personal enmity, but it was probably also influenced by his relationship with John Wigan, who was a preacher at Birch's chapel in Rusholme, Manchester, in the 1640s. Wigan had a special interest in the college building because he had established a Baptist chapel in part of the complex, and he and Captain Jeffrey Ellison petitioned the Committee for Compounding with Delinquents. A survey was carried out which suggests that the Baptist meeting room may have been re-established within the main building complex:

> The large building called the Colledge in Manchester consisting of many rooms with two barns, one gatehouse very much decayed, one parcel of

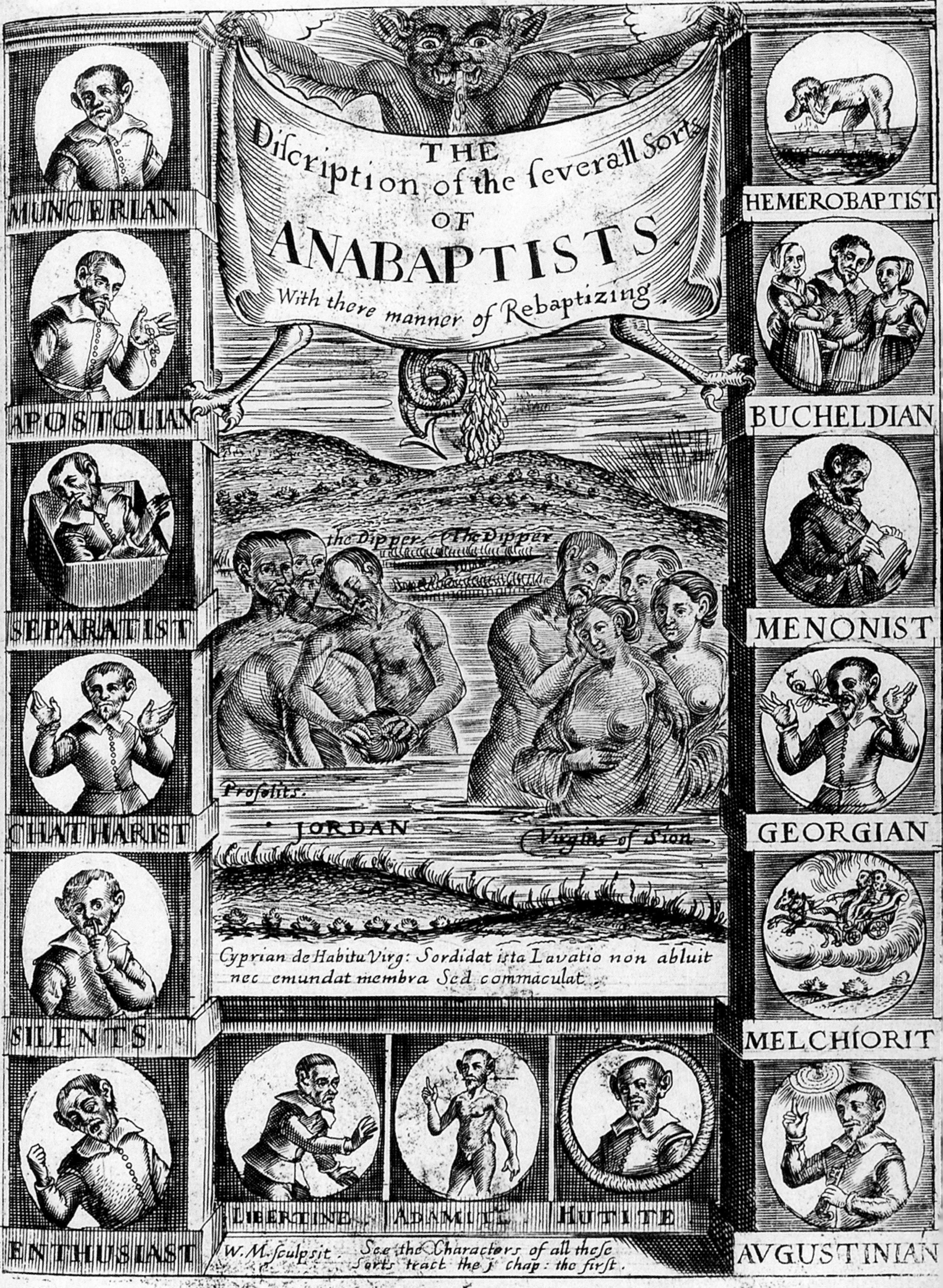
THE
Discription of the severall Sorts
OF
ANABAPTISTS.
With there manner of Rebaptizing.
MUNCERIAN
APOSTOLIAN
SEPARATIST
CHATHARIST
SILENTS.
ENTHUSIAST
HEMEROBAPTIST
BUCHELDIAN
MENONIST
GEORGIAN
MELCHIORIT
AVGUSTINIAN
the Dipper
The Dipper
Prosolits.
JORDAN
Virgins of Sion
Cyprian de Habitu Virg: Sordidat ista Lavatio non abluit nec emundat membra Sed commaculat.
LIBERTINE
ADAMITE
HUTITE
W.M. sculpsit. See the Characters of all these Sorts tract the 5 chap: the first.

> ground formerly an orchard and one garden now in the possession of Joseph Werden gent who pays for the use of the Common £10 yearly. There is likewise one other room in the said college repaired and now made use for publique meetings of Christian conscientious people. All of which we conceive to be worth to be let for seven years the clear yearly rent of ten pounds.[54]

The pair obtained a seven-year lease on the buildings in 1653, the year of Chetham's death. At that time the property belonged to the dowager Countess, who was subsequently allowed to recover her estates, including the college, on payment of a fine of £7,200. This did not affect the agreement, as terms for the surrender of this part of the estate had already been reached with her by Wigan and Ellison.[55]

John Wigan (d. 1665) introduced congregational principles to the chapel at Birch where he was curate in 1644. He subsequently became an Anabaptist and Fifth Monarchist and is credited with being responsible for bringing these radical ideas to Cheshire and the Manchester area.[56] According to Adam Martindale, who was writing in 1649–50:

> The colledge lands being sold, and the colledge itself to Mr Wigan, who now being turned Antipaedobaptist and I know not what more, made a barn there into a chappell, where he and many of his perswasion preached doctrine diametrically opposite to the ministers under their very nose.[57]

The rejection of infant baptism was repugnant to moderate Puritans and the strict separatism and anti-authoritarianism of Baptist sects was considered dangerous and seditious. Daniel Featley, author of a polemical tract of 1645 called *The Dippers Dipt* (Fig. 42), noted: 'in one Anabaptist you have many Heretiques, and in this one Sect . . . many erroneous and schismaticall positions and practises'.[58] It is thought that Wigan may have developed his radical views through contact with the New Model Army, which was campaigning in Lancashire in 1648.[59] In 1851 he became a captain in the Army and his acquisition of the lease of the college buildings can be seen as an attempt to ensure that the Manchester Baptist congregation was guaranteed a meeting place.

42. Frontispiece of Daniel Featley's polemical anti-baptist tract *The Dippers Dipt* showing various different groups of Baptists condemned by Featley with a suggestive scene of adult baptism. By permission of the British Library, E268 (11)

CHAPTER FOUR

'A Masterpiece of Bounty'

The Creation of Chetham's Hospital and Library

When Humphrey Chetham died on 22 September 1653, aged seventy-two, the value of his estate was estimated to be £13,897 1*s.* 2*d.* – a huge sum for that period. His will, made in 1651, provided unusually large sums for the support of the charity; £500 for the purchase of a suitable building for his library and hospital project, £100 for library furnishings, £1,000 for books and £7,000 for the purchase of lands to generate an income for the institution. Forty boys were to be maintained and educated, then apprenticed at the age of fourteen. Later

43. Detail of Fig. 40

44. The chained library provided for Gorton parish church under the terms of Chetham's will

in the seventeenth century the bequest was described by Thomas Fuller, who called it 'as great a Masterpiece of Bounty, as our age hath afforded'.[60]

In addition to the main provisions of the will, Chetham directed that five chained libraries consisting of 'godly English Bookes' were to be provided for local churches and chapels. Of these two survive, one at Turton Tower, near Bolton, and another made for Gorton parish church, in east Manchester (Fig. 44). This is now owned by Chetham's Library and can be seen in the library reading room complete with the original chained books. Described as 'one of the most interesting . . . of the English libraries which preserve their chains',[61] the library is in the form of an almery, or book chest, a popular way of storing books during the medieval period, when the practice of chaining books had its origins.

Before school or library could be set up the problem of where it was to be housed remained. Despite the fact that the college building was now in the hands of Wigan and Ellison, it was still an attractive proposition. It was situated in the centre of town, and adaptation for use by the charity would be relatively straightforward. In any event Chetham's will had made it clear that using the college building was his preferred option: 'And my desire is that the great howse . . . in Manchester aforesaid, called the colledge or the colledge house, may be purchased and bought for the same purpose (if it may be hadd, and obteyned upon good termes and for a good estate)'.[62] The feoffees, appointed by Chetham, offered £350 for it, but this was rejected and they raised the amount to £400 in a meeting held on 24 January 1653/4.[63] After more delays Ellison and Wigan accepted their offer, and Charles, eighth Earl of Derby, was paid £30 for his consent, and signed an indenture later that year.[64] After the Restoration it became necessary to negotiate directly with the heirs of the Earl, and a lease for the period of ninety-nine years was obtained from Charlotte, Countess of Derby for a peppercorn rent in 1660.[65]

It was presumably at the time of the negotiations with Wigan and Ellison that the feoffees commissioned their own survey which was undertaken by Richard Martinscrofte, a surveyor, mathematician and joiner, and a group of local masons, carpenters and joiners.[66] This estimated the value of the buildings, which included a number of ancillary structures since demolished, to be £5310 10*s.* 8*d.* making the purchase price of £400 seem a bargain, especially as it was sufficiently large to accommodate the library and hospital, with room to spare which could generate income by being rented out. It seems likely that Martinscrofte's valuation was based on estimates for the cost of replacing all the buildings and contents from scratch, rather than representing the actual market value. The poor condition of the buildings was perhaps also a consideration in fixing the sale price, and it is doubtful if Wigan and Ellison

45. The inner side of the gatehouse. It was extensively repaired in the 1650s, and is one of the few parts of the building to escape refacing in the nineteenth century

would have had the funds to put the buildings into good order, whereas the terms of Chetham's will made ample provision for this.

The work of repairing and fitting out the building for its new purposes represented a huge undertaking which could never have been completed without the determination, dedication and hard work of the executors and feoffees. The work had to be planned and co-ordinated, raw materials obtained, and the teams of craftsmen and their labourers hired and supervised. Arrangements had to be made for appointing staff and providing for the needs of the boys, as well as obtaining books for the library. On top of all this there were various legal matters to deal with and the question of investing Chetham's bequest in property and arranging to administer it. Chetham's nephew Edward Chetham, James Lightbowne, and Thomas Minshull were among those who had a close involvement in the work. The Lightbownes of Moston, north Manchester, had been friends and close associates, and James's brother, John was Chetham's lawyer. Minshull was an apothecary, and Chetham's physician. Other feoffees included his close friends Richard Johnson, John Tildsley and Richard Hollingworth, influential Presbyterian divines, of whom Hollingworth was a fellow of the college and an antiquarian, who wrote a history of Manchester in the mid 1650s. Others were drawn from the local gentry, including members of the Mosley, Worsley and Barlow families. The choice of men, who included some ex-royalists among a majority of Parliamentarians and Presbyterians, perhaps reflects a desire to unite merchants and gentry, and to promote social cohesion in the aftermath of the war, or as a recent study has put it: 'Including both ex-royalists and Parliamentarians amongst his charitable feoffees was just one small way of reuniting the body politic in Lancashire.'[67]

CONVERSION AND REPAIR OF THE BUILDING

Work evidently began soon after the sale had taken place. Initial repairs had been completed by November 1655 when the feoffees resolved 'That the great gatehouse and the rest of the colledge not repaired may be viewed and considered of and how to repare the same, and to rent that part thereof that may be well spared' (Fig. 45).[68] By the middle of 1656 matters were sufficiently advanced to allow the admission of forty boys.[69]

First records of repairs appear in a document entitled 'Moneys disbursed about the Colledge Business',[70] a tally of various different sums expended between June 1653 and May 1656. Two payments of twenty pounds were made during this period to James Lightbowne 'towards the repaire of the Colledge', and another payment of twenty pounds for the same purpose went to Richard Dutton. In addition to this thirteen loads of lime were paid for in August 1654 and twelve

loads of slates paid for in October of that year. It looks as if these supplies must have been used to repair the cloistral ranges, which were the first parts of the building to be restored. Richard Dutton was appointed as the first house governor, or headmaster, of the hospital in 1655. He had a salary of twenty pounds, and his duties included keeping accounts of expenditure and helping to organise provision of the household equipment needed. His accounts, which are set out in Appendix 5, begin with an entry for 25 July 1656 and cover the period up to 10 April 1658.[71] Pages at the beginning and at the end are missing but much valuable information can be obtained.

Contrary to the usual assumption, they show that work was far from complete when the hospital was dedicated by Richard Hollingworth in August 1656. The boys admitted at that time spent their first year or so in the midst of a bustling building site. A vivid picture of activity is painted, with masons, bricklayers, carpenters, glaziers, and plasterers hard at work supplied by a seemingly endless procession of carts carrying flags, slates, sand, stone and other raw materials to the site. Tasks mentioned include levelling and flagging floors, slating roofs,

46. The 'boyes Cloathes'. The traditional charity school uniform of tunic, pancake cap, stockings and buckled shoes hardly changed from the seventeenth century until its use was discontinued in the twentieth century. Here the boys are taking part in the annual Founder's Day ceremony

laying board floors, and mending or installing new casements before fitting glass. Men were painting and 'trimminge' rooms as they were completed, and women were employed to clean up afterwards. Payments for drink for the workmen are recorded on several occasions.

Meanwhile household equipment, bedding and furniture had to be bought or made. In the summer of 1656 preparations were being made for the admission of the boys. Bowls for 'the boys to wash in' were bought, and a tailor, John Curtis, was paid for making bolsters and blankets for them. 'Catachisms' bought by James Lightbowne helped to provide for their spiritual welfare, and in September of that year George Walker was paid for 'mendinge the boyes Cloathes' (Fig. 46).

More than eighty different people were involved in the building work, many identified by name in the accounts. The principal craftsmen were the exotically named carpenter, Hercules Chadwicke; the mason Edward Platt; plasterer Henry Walker; glazier William Williamson; and Ralph and Richard Smith, bricklayers. Richard Martinscrofte and his son George were the joiners responsible for building the library shelves, and they almost certainly made some of the furniture. The carpenter was on the highest pay, at 1*s.* 6*d.* per day, while the mason received 1*s.* 4*d.* The Martinscroftes earned 1*s.* 2*d.* per day, the bricklayer 1*s.* 2*d.* and the plasterer 1*s.* The slater, Richard Karsley, was paid by the yard, and the glazier was paid per window.

Many of the men were residents of Manchester and appear in lists of inhabitants made by the constables of the town in the mid-seventeenth century.[72] From this source we learn that Edward Platt was living in Toad Lane (Todd Street), Humphrey Peacock the cooper, Peter Dickson the timber merchant, and Ralph Wollen, who supplied clasps for the books, all lived on Long Millgate, while Thurstan Diggle had a house on St Mary's Gate. Williamson, Diggle and Platt served as officers of the Court Leet, though the multiplicity of these unpaid posts perhaps made this an unwelcome duty rather than an honour.

Some idea of the scale of the operation is given by the quantities of materials used during this time. More than two hundred feet of glass and six hundred and seventy glass quarries (small square or diamond panes) were paid for. At least forty loads of flagstones were brought from Rochdale, and seventy loads of lime and thirty-one loads of slate were used. Quantities of sand were delivered, some of it from 'Broughton Foard'. Supplies of nails, lead, and hair to bind the plaster are among other items mentioned. As the work progressed around 700 loads of 'rubbadge' were removed from the yard at a penny a load. The large quantities of lime purchased and many references to 'shootering', [shuttering], 'teereing' [daubing] and 'whiteing' suggest that the plaster ceilings

47. Entrance in the south cloister. The circular hole at the base of the door gave cats access to the room

concealing the medieval roof timbers, which survived in many parts of the building until the late nineteenth century, were put up at this time. This expedient would have presumably cut down draughts and made the rooms easier to heat.

There are many references to making new doors, and fitting them with locks, usually supplied by Thurstan Diggle and Jeremy Woosencrofte, but where they were serviceable the original medieval doors were retained, and many survive today. A glimpse of domestic conditions is given by the holes cut into the lower part of many of them, allowing cats to move about the building to control the inevitable population of rodents (Fig. 47), though we cannot be sure when this was done. The doors of the building could be a study in themselves, exhibiting as they do a treasure trove of seventeenth-century fittings and locks.

A brick wall was erected to divide the courtyard from a garden where men were paid for 'seting stoopes [posts] and railes'. The ample space was to prove useful for playing games and contrasted with the tiny yard of the then adjacent Manchester Grammar School, which was described as 'very unwholesome in the summer tyme by reason of the many schollers and want of aire and roome'.[73] The school later sought, and received, permission to allow its pupils to use Chetham's yard for sports activities.

Funds were available for something beyond mere function. Two sundials are mentioned in the accounts on several occasions during the summer of 1657. Described as the 'great dyall' and the 'little dyall', one of them could be that shown on the south face of the porch in John Palmer's drawing (Fig. 17). Richard Martinscrofte set them out, and more than six shillings was spent on gold and nearly as much on labour for gilding as well as nearly three shillings on 'payntinge stuffe and oyle for the Diall'.

THE LIBRARY

The west cloister range seems to have been the first part of the building to be converted. A building designed to accommodate a small community did not require much change to make it suitable as a school, but the way in which the library was incorporated would have had to be given thought. The idea of converting the upper fellows' rooms was perhaps suggested by the ease of removing light timber-framed partitions there, and the long narrow ranges thus created may have chimed with memories of college libraries at Oxford and Cambridge for those of the feoffees who had been university men, seven in all. Lawyer Robert Booth, for example, had attended St John's College Cambridge, Nicholas Mosley had been at Magdalene College, Cambridge and Richard Holland at Brasenose College, Oxford. The first librarian, appointed in 1656, was Robert Browne who had been educated at Emmanuel College, Cambridge. The libraries at St John's College (started in 1596) and Merton College (1373–8) in Oxford resemble the library at Chetham's in that they also occupy two long rooms at right angles to one another at first-floor level.

Richard Martinscrofte was responsible for building the shelves, chaining the books and making the library stools (Fig. 48). It must have been he and his son who made much of the furniture for the feoffees' rooms.[74] He came from a Scottish Roman Catholic family and was baptised on 10 April 1606 in

Manchester, where he spent the rest of his life. In the Court Leet records, where he is frequently listed as a minor official, Martinscrofte is described as a joiner but he built up a considerable reputation as a mathematical surveyor and as a teacher of mathematics. He made a number of maps for local gentry families in the 1640s when the progress of the Civil War made it expedient for landowners to make a record of their holdings. What experience Martinscrofte had of libraries is not known, although his gravestone in Eccles church claims that he became remarkable for his skill in decorating arks, chests and cabinets. In addition to the work at Chetham's, Martinscrofte was responsible for making the Boroughreeve's chest for the town archives. As far as the library interior is concerned it seems likely that he had a virtually free hand. According to the accounts, between 2 August 1656 and 13 November 1657, he put in sixty-seven-and-a-half days' labour, while his son George put in thirty-nine days, and their labourer worked for forty days at a shilling a day. In addition Martinscrofte the elder received ale, for which Ann Rawsthorne was paid two shillings in September 1656, while another payment of three shillings was made for his ale the following December.

Chained libraries might be in the form of an almery, as with the Gorton library, or on the desk or lectern system, where the books were laid flat on reading desks. The introduction of a stall, or shelf system, and the innovation of placing the books on end and then chaining them, probably originated in the fifteenth century and continued into the eighteenth century. This was the method used at Chetham's. The original book presses, or shelves, are of oak, and on average they are ten feet long, two feet wide and seven feet high. They are of the three-decker type with three sections on each side divided by two uprights to give nine compartments. They were raised to create more shelf space during the eighteenth century, and originally they would have allowed a great deal more light to enter.

After the shelves had been made much of the work involved fixing clasps on the books and chaining them, in accordance with the instructions in the founder's will. The accounts itemise many payments for chains, rods and clasps. Some of the equipment came from Wigan, then a centre for armourer's shops, but most of it was provided by local suppliers named in the accounts as Laurence Garner, Ralph Wollen, Jeremy Woosencrofte and John Whitehead. Brass for clasps was purchased on four occasions, a total of seventeen and a quarter pounds weight at a cost of £1 1*s*. 4*d*., which produced almost 1,500 clasps. The chains were bought from Henry Pierson, a Manchester smith, some forty dozen being purchased at 4*s*. per dozen. Locks for the library door and desks were bought, while eighteen locks for presses (bookshelves) were supplied by Jeremy Woosencrofte at a cost of 2*s*. 6*d*. each. Woosencrofte was also the main supplier

Overleaf: 48. The library west range, showing the shelves and stools made by Richard Martinscrofte

X
Lexica et

of iron rods, in addition to which he supplied several long iron pins, stubs and sockets, all for chaining the books.

The policy of continuing acquisition of books, provided for in Chetham's will, means that the process of chaining was an ongoing one, and this is perhaps what Martinscrofte was doing when a local diarist records that he was working in the library in 1661.[75] Chaining was not discontinued until the middle of the eighteenth century.

In 1665 the feoffees ordered that: 'the Great chamber and closett being on the South of the said hospital betwixt the library and the ffeoffees chamber bee made uniforme to the library.'[76] This seems to relate to the rooms on the south side of the cloister, the present south library range. The expression 'bee made uniforme' is difficult to interpret, and could simply be a reference to the reopening of the doorway between the chamber and library. Alternatively it might refer to wholesale conversion, implying that initially the library had only occupied the west range. Expenditure was unusually high in that year, with the treasurer authorising payments of £1341 15*s.* 11*d.*[77] as compared with sums of £542 8*s.* 8*d.* the following year and similar sums in following and immediately preceding years. The need for more space for the ever-increasing numbers of books was probably the reason. The terms of the charity provided for annual sums to be spent on books, many of which were bought in London. Initially the principal supplier was the second-hand bookseller Robert Littlebury of Little Britain. The library also regularly received gifts of books and manuscripts. It may well be that the intention had always been to use the space for the library but the actual work of conversion was delayed until the need became pressing, or the finances available.

ACCESS AND CIRCULATION

The alterations involved a reorganisation of circulation to provide new points of access to the library and to private staff rooms. A new entrance was made to the library from the north so that visitors gained entrance from Hunts Bank either from a route near the bridge over the River Irk (Fig. 49) or from the other end near the church. This was described as late as 1826 as being the main entrance, except for carriages.[78] A covered corridor, probably the structure described as a porch in the building accounts, was built at the north-west corner of the building and external stairs led up to a flat leaded roof over the corridor, described by Celia Fiennes, who wrote: 'out of the library there are leads on which one has the sight of the town.'[79] An entrance to the library from this upper level was made by re-using a medieval doorway removed when the internal wall was knocked through. The corridor is a curious structure, with a

roof of great angled slabs and slit windows. At the north end, where there are lavatories, the roof is of large re-used timbers with sixteenth- or seventeenth-century mouldings. On the exterior wall an abraded carving probably acted as a gargoyle originally.

A new stair tower was placed at the north east corner of the cloister courtyard reusing the original entrance to the space. The handsome stair, with its decorative timber balusters (Fig. 50), provided a stylish approach to the rooms over the pantry and buttery used as the private quarters of the house governor, and the upper rooms beside them, the quarters of the librarian. The stone steps have a stone string with a wooden balustrade, probably made by the Martinscroftes, typical of the sort of work one would expect to find in a minor gentry house of this period. There are pierced and shaped splat balusters, and newel posts with decorative carving. On the landing the original window opening of the cloister is also fitted with balusters. The stairwell is lit by medieval windows, one of which must have been salvaged from the upper part of the cloister, but it is not clear where the other one came from, unless it was a lower hall window. The upper hall window on this side was retained and borrows light from the hall.

49. The north side of the building with the River Irk in the foreground in an engraving of 1823. On the right is the covered corridor constructed by Edward Platt's team, with steps leading from it down to the riverside. The river was culverted in the nineteenth century

50. Seventeenth-century stair leading to the private quarters of the house governor and the librarian

An entrance at the west end of the north cloister walkway leads into the library (Fig. 51). The original medieval opening has been reduced in size, and grotesque carving above the door could be of sixteenth- or seventeenth-century date, probably inserted during the conversion work. It is likely that this route was

51. Doorway from the library to the north cloister walkway

designed for use by staff and special visitors, with others expected to use the entrance from Hunts Bank, so avoiding library visitors entering the main body of the building.

52. The Audit Room

FEOFFEES' ROOMS

The warden's lodgings, at the south end of the hall, were designated for use by the feoffees. The lower room came to be known as the Audit Room, as business meetings and the yearly audit took place there (Fig. 52). The elaborate plasterwork here consists of a trail design, a little like a crude version of the sixteenth-century plasterwork at Speke Hall in Liverpool.[80] On the whole it seems likely that it was carried out during the seventeenth-century conversion, although the design would be conservative for that date, and the appearance of Chetham's arms over the fireplace seems to confirm this. Although there is no reference to decorative plasterwork in the seventeenth-century accounts or minutes, Henry Walker the plasterer was busy at work in the room during April 1657, when he was paid for twenty-nine days work there; the amount of time spent is a good indication that it must have been done then. Before the plastering started the medieval timber ceiling required attention. Jeremy Woosencrofte was paid for '2 great Iron pinns for the broken beam in the great parlour' on 6 March 1656/7, a repair clearly visible today. The panelling and doors also date from this period, including a little entrance lobby, and there is an impressive array of door fittings including cockshead hinges (Fig. 53) and an intricate brass latch and plate.

53. Detail of a door in the Audit Room with cockshead hinges, so-called for their distinctive shape

The upper room was described by Celia Fiennes as the feoffees' dining room and was still used for that purpose in the nineteenth century. Work in this area, described as the 'great Chamber' in the building accounts, was underway in March 1657/8. It included 'making window stooles . . . and cuting the Arch beames feete'. This is a reference to removing part of the medieval roof timbers which originally extended down the walls. They were probably cut off so that the room could be panelled, work which seems to have been undertaken later that month. Thurstan Diggle was paid for '4 pairs of bands, latches and catches for the seeled doores', and many of these survive. New glass was put in and the windows repaired, and the finishing touches were being made in March when payments are made for 'layinge coloures' using material supplied by Ralphe Wollen.

The splendid carved tympanum which occupies part of the north wall of the room was inserted at a later date, perhaps in the early eighteenth century, though it is not known exactly when it was executed. It is very striking, with unusual motifs and carving of great vigour. It is obviously a memorial to Chetham, however no record of it has been found in any of the surviving documents. The fact that Celia Fiennes does not mention it suggests that it might post-date her visit, as one would expect a visitor who was given a tour of the building to be shown such a splendid addition to the establishment and to be sufficiently impressed to record it. The feoffees did discuss commissioning a statue of Chetham in 1675–6,[81] a project which did not get off the ground until an ex-pupil commissioned the marble monument by William Theed in Manchester Cathedral in 1853 (Fig. 4). The only other clue appears in an entry in the minutes for 5 October 1747 when mention is made of panelling or decorating the south side of the room, but this does not represent a very likely lead since the tympanum is actually on the north side of the room, and the work would be very old fashioned for 1747.

The carving occupies all the available space in the north wall between wall plate level and the arch braces of the roof timbers (Fig. 55). The composition is framed by an arched band with a pecked ground, repeating floral motifs and raised scrolls at the edges. Within it there is an array of symbolic motifs framed by flowing acanthus leaf designs. In the centre Chetham's arms have foliated mantling surmounted by a helm, with his motto below, the whole sitting on a pile of books supported by a foliated bracket which is carved to look like a grotesque face. Above, a big squat eagle grasps ropes of foliage and flowers which extend on each side of the arms and terminate with drapery drops twined with flowers. The five-petalled flowers at the base of the drop are of the type invented by Grinling Gibbons and used at St Paul's Cathedral, London. On either side wreathed obelisks rise from piles of books on foliated brackets and support shell

54. The great chamber, now the library reading room

lamps. Finally, flanking the obelisks, birds; on one side the pelican in her piety, on the other a remarkably vigorous cockerel grasping ears of corn in its claws against a tree or bush which is almost equally remarkable for the crudeness of execution. The contrast here is so great that the possibility that the cockerel is a later restoration cannot be discounted. The quality of the carving does vary within the piece, however, suggesting it was the product of more than one hand in a workshop. The central arms and the mantling, for example, are better quality work than many of the other elements. Paint and varnish, probably introduced in the nineteenth century, make it difficult to be certain what type of wood has been used, but a recent examination suggests it is lime wood,[82] which would be consistent with English carving practice in the late seventeenth and early eighteenth centuries.

The iconography is not difficult to decipher. The Solomonic obelisks and lamps are symbols of wisdom and learning. The pelican with her young is a symbol of Christian sacrifice, while the cockerel could be a symbol of Mercury and a reference to Chetham's successful career as a merchant. The use of books as part of the design has parallels in sixteenth- and seventeenth-century funerary monuments. The scholar monument, with the subject treated as an upright half-effigy reading, teaching or preaching, sometimes with books incorporated into

55. The tympanum in the reading room. English Heritage

the design, is a type found from the 1570s to the 1620s. The memorial to Thomas Bodley (d. 1613) by Nicholas Stone in Merton College Chapel, Oxford, shows the librarian surrounded by his books. A number of memorials in other Oxford colleges incorporate books[83] and some seventeenth-century bishops were commemorated by recumbent effigies surrounded by stacks of books, including Archbishop Abbot of Canterbury, Archbishop Frewen of York, and Bishop Dove of Peterborough.

It is difficult to suggest a date and designer for such a piece. It is clearly the work of carvers familiar with the work of Grinling Gibbons. It is lively and parts are well drawn, but it is far below the quality of the work (almost certainly by Gibbons) at Lyme Hall, Cheshire, or Samuel Watson's carving at Chatsworth, Derbyshire, to mention two local examples. The design must have been drawn up in consultation with someone who had a very clear idea of the qualities and attributes which should be portrayed, but there is no reason to suppose that it is not the work of a local firm which had absorbed the fashions and conventions disseminated by Gibbons' workshop.

An inventory of 1671 with additions of 1681[84] must be the one which Richard Dutton was asked to make that records 'all the Goods that are within and doe belong unto the Hospitall'.[85] It would have been one of his last jobs, since he died the following month. The document mentions the dining chamber (library reading room) with three tables and '24 back chaires leathered' and the parlour (Audit Room) with three tables and twelve chairs. The accounts list a payment made on 24 April 1657 for 'dressing and colouring redd three dozen calf skins', perhaps for the leather upholstering of the chairs. If so the present upholstering in red leather reproduces the original, and if one skin per chair is allowed this tallies with the thirty-six chairs mentioned in the inventory. These chairs, probably made by Martinscrofte, are of oak with turned legs and a stretcher between the front legs carved with scroll work.

The unusual and impressive tables in the reading room were probably also Martinscrofte's work. The enormous size of the two larger ones means that they must have been assembled in the room, as they are far too big to fit through any of the doorways. The gate-leg table in the centre of the reading room is thought to be one of the largest of its type in England, measuring over seven foot seven by six foot one. Two other tables have legs treated as carved consoles, thought to be an unusually early use of a motif derived from Continental examples, and described by one source as combining 'a type of construction evolved in Elizabethan times with a form that was a favourite one of William Kent'.[86] The larger of the two (Fig. 56) has arcading between the pairs of legs in the form of pierced balusters of the type often seen in staircases of the date.

Payments were made in November 1656 for 'seeleing in' the hall, probably work of preparing the false ceiling which covered the original roof, and the room was flagged by Edward Platt and his team in December. Plastering had started there in April of the following year and was continued during the summer. A carpenter was at work 'layinge sleepers at the upp[er] end of the hall to board on' in January 1657/8 and flooring was installed in March. Considering the amount of work this represents it is interesting that a decision was made to retain the traditional high table arrangement, with a dais. The hospital staff would have used it when dining and to preside over communal events, while the children used 'the boyes long table in tow'. There were forms, stools and cushions, two bibles, and 'one desk for the great bible'.

56. One of the reading room tables, probably made by Richard Martinscrofte in the 1650s. Country Life Picture Library

The boys used the ground floor rooms off the cloister immediately below the library. The inventory suggests that they occupied six rooms at six or eight to a room, assuming that they each had a bed. They had blankets, bolsters, sheets and a shared towel, and there were pewter chamber pots, yellow rugs and chests. This would have represented great luxury to children who came from very impoverished homes, where there would have been little room and few comforts.

The House Governor Richard Dutton had the suite of rooms on the north side of the hall over the buttery and pantry and the room over the porch, still used as the private quarters of the head teacher today. The spy holes made in the walls giving views of the hall and kitchen were probably provided at this time so that he could keep an eye on activities there. The one to the hall survives with a timber surround on the hall side and a door with original hinges on the other side. The rooms had probably also been refurbished at an early stage, and no mention is made of them in the accounts, though the inventory mentions a pair of beds. Other furniture would probably have been Dutton's own.

The college silver was kept in a trunk in Dutton's room, and the inventory mentions '2 colledg potts, 2 kanns, too tumblers, 2 bouls, 2 salts, 6 little salts two dossin of spoons, and 2 wine cupps that was made of one of the tumblers'.

57. Part of the collection of college silver which includes items acquired in the 1670s. The ox-eye cups are shown on the extreme left and right of the picture

58. Rooms beside the gatehouse were probably those let out to Alexander Greene, where he had a brew house

This description is probably one of the amendments made to the inventory in 1681, since some of these items can be identified with silver owned by the institution today, including pieces bought after 1671 (Fig. 57). The present collection includes seventeen tablespoons of 1667, which must be the survivors of '24 silver spoons strong and plaine' ordered by the feoffees in 1667,[87] two standing cups of *c.* 1670, two vases of 1674, six salt cellars of 1674 and a basin of similar date. At least four smiths were responsible, and other examples of their work have been identified at Oriel College, Oxford, St Paul's Shadwell, London, and Christ's College, Cambridge. The two vases, or ox-eye cups, were made in 1674 by a court goldsmith who made plate for St George's Chapel, Windsor, and Kensington Palace Chapel.[88] These pieces have the initials AC and the maker could have been the Huguenot smith Augustine Courtauld.[89] The silver is an exceptional collection in unusually good condition. The pewter plates and dishes recorded in the buttery and kitchen would have served everyday purposes.

Rooms for some of the other members of staff were nearing completion in the summer of 1656, as works of 'trimminge' the cook's and librarian's rooms are mentioned and payments for 'paintinge stuffe' and 'Ash Coloure for triminge the Cookes Chamber' are made. The librarian, Mr Browne, had the upper room on the north range immediately beside the library, where in October 1656 Ralph Smith was paid for 'making an hobb and setting a fyre iron'.

KITCHEN AND SERVICE ROOMS

The kitchen floor was flagged in December 1657, and although there are few other references to the room, frequent payments were made for kitchen and cellar equipment. The inventory lists an impressive array of gear for cooking and food preparation, including brass vessels, toasting irons, various 'hacking' 'shreading' and 'strikeing' knives, 'dreeping panns' and a 'kneading trough'. The cellar was also well-equipped, with seven barrels, three half barrels and two hogsheads.

Other rooms mentioned in the inventory include the 'Treasurer', where accounts and money were kept, and the 'cookes chamber' and 'Womans parlor'. The latter suggests that a woman may have been employed to help to look after the boys, some of whom were under ten years old. The wives of house governors seem often to have fulfilled this function in later years.

Some of the rooms in the range east of the kitchen were let out. In 1661 it was agreed to lease the 'chamber over the gatehouse' to Edward Chetham.[90] On 6 October 1658 a decision was made 'That Mr Alexander Greene have the 3

59. Watercolour of 1819 of the House of Correction by Thomas Barritt, based on an earlier view

chambers and the bruehowse and the stables . . . for and during the span and time of ten years'.[91] It is possible that this regularised or renewed an arrangement which preceded the acquisition of the building, since a brewhouse is said to have been set up in the college building by 1650, when the brewers were presented at the court of the Duchy of Lancaster for refusing to grind their malt at the mill owned by the Grammar School.[92] Greene was a well known local vintner who lived on St Mary's Gate. He acted as a senior constable during the 1640s and 1650s and it was at his house that early meetings of the feoffees were held, and more famously, where one of the first of the Civil War skirmishes in Manchester started.[93]

There are several references in the minutes to Greene, who appears not to have paid his rent regularly, and the feoffees ordered that the 'room called the stable' should be converted into a schoolroom in 1663[94] but the conversion was not carried out immediately. Richard Dutton was ordered to demand the return of rooms from Greene in 1665,[95] which might be the date of their conversion for use by the school. The angled range beside the gatehouse and the rooms beside it were almost certainly those rented by him and the 'newe

Chamber over the Brewehouse' mentioned in the inventory was perhaps fitted up for use by the school after the rooms were taken back. Early nineteenth-century drawings (Fig. 66) show obvious signs of alteration and rebuilding in this area which may reflect repairs done by Greene or alterations undertaken for the school after he left.

ANCILLARY BUILDINGS

The sale of the college had included a number of buildings which have since disappeared. A survey made *c.* 1654 by Richard Martinscrofte and others[96] was presumably drawn up at around the time of the purchase of the building by Chetham's executors. Some or all of the buildings described could have been part of the original fifteenth-century complex.

'The Haye Barne we esteem to be worth as It now stands the sum of	£167
The Corne Barne we value to be worth with the comon stable adioyning	£541 4*s.*
The Inner housinge – The Gate house upon the East side	£143 4*s.*
The building being all of stone betweene The stable and the Hall door Eastward from the Hall	£641 4*s.*
The outside from the Hall doore to the water being likewise of stonework	£1546
The Gate house Westward	£279 12*s.*
The Washe House	£118 16*s.*
The Garden Wall	£220
The Slaughter house	£13 6*s.* 8*d.*
The side Ile after the wall between the Stable and the Hall	£10
Summa Totalis	£5310 10*s.* 8*d.*

Some of these buildings are referred to in other sources. One of the barns had been fitted up by John Wigan as a Baptist chapel in 1649 or 1650, possibly the little barn, or hay barn, which was initially excluded from the sale. The larger corn barn was described in a deed reproduced in the Court Leet records as being forty yards long and about ten and a half yards wide with a four-bay dwelling house attached to it.[97] Described in seventeenth-century leases and releases as the 'Greate Barn', it was subsequently sold for use as a house of correction. The minutes of 6 April 1656 record:

> 'That the executors may sell Rawsthornes howse, the greate barn and the cort as it is meered [marked out] forth unto the justices or whom they may appoint for the sum of one hundred and twenty pounds, the same to be for a howse of correction and workehowse.'[98]

A statute of 1575 directed that a house of correction should be built in every county for punishing rogues, vagabonds and other undesirables. The first mention of such an establishment in Manchester appears in the constables' accounts for 1615–16 when money was received for the building of a facility and paid to Oswald Mosley.[99] It is not clear where this building was sited, and little more is known about it. It may be that the plans for it had come to nothing, or that a larger building was needed by the 1650s. The fact that it was also described as a workhouse suggests that it was also used to house parish paupers under the provisions of the Poor Law Act of 1601 which regularised the administration of relief for the poor which had originally been provided for in an Act of 1536.

The building is shown in a watercolour (Fig. 59), with the people inside hanging pots out of the windows to beg for food or alms. It looks as if the building in the foreground is the four-bay house belonging to Rawsthorne, while the one behind with timber-framing shown in the gable could have been the barn. Edward Rawsthorne is listed as a resident in the Hunts Bank area in 1641–2[100] and Ann Rawsthorne, who was paid for ale provided for Richard Martinscrofte in September 1656, was presumably a relative. There are several seventeenth- and eighteenth-century references to the house of correction. An account of 1783 states that at that time it had recently been rebuilt, and describes cells cut down into the sandstone 'aired by funnels'.[101] The building may have continued in use as an inn until the Palatine Buildings were erected in the 1840s.[102]

The exact position of the 'Gatehouse westward' is unclear, but it is probably identifiable with the college gate 'towards Hunt Hall' described by John Dee in 1598 when it was damaged in a storm.[103] It is mentioned in several leases and deeds from this period. A deed of 1664[104] relating to the sale of the college buildings by Wigan and Ellison shows that this gatehouse and the 'little barn' as well as a small portion of land was excluded from the sale. The gatehouse is described thus:

> 'one building standinge by itt self called the Gate house situate and standing toward the Church yard att the upper end of one street or place in Manchester aforesaid called the hunts bank [this lies beneath present day Victoria Street]'.

Wigan evidently still owned or occupied this gatehouse which is described in a lease of 1657 as: 'the College gate house towards the church now in the occupacion of John Wigan Clerk.'[105] Unfortunately little is known of the subsequent history of the building and any evidence for its exact position was probably destroyed during the nineteenth century when the street level was raised or during construction of the Palatine Buildings.

The hay barn was the 'litle barne and one other building at the end of it towards one streete in Manchester called the Millnegate' described in a release of 1654,[106] one of the buildings retained by Wigan, perhaps for continued use as a Baptist meeting room. What subsequently happened to it is not known, and the fate of the slaughterhouse and wash house also remains unclear. The minutes record in a rather sad little entry on 5 November 1655 'That the executors desyne to remoove those persons inhabiting within the school court viz Joe Bullocke, his wyfe and childe and also Alice Deane and her daughter and the said habitacions be taken down and made use of for the repair of the hospital.' Presumably these families had made homes in some of the buildings listed in the survey, or perhaps they had dwellings too humble to be mentioned in that document. A John Bullocke is listed as living in the area in 1648 and 1651, and he was employed by the Court Leet on several occasions to guard the town lock up.[107]

INCORPORATION AND EXPANSION AFTER THE CONVERSION

By the close of the 1650s the work of repairing and adapting the building was substantially complete. The first forty boys had been there for several years and the pattern of life for both school and library must have been fairly well established. Soon afterwards the feoffees decided to act upon Chetham's testamentary instruction to obtain a charter of incorporation. In 1662 Richard Johnson and Edward Chetham were instructed to go to London in pursuit of the aim.[108] Negotiations were prolonged, but eventually Charles II granted the charter in 1665, which incorporated the charity into a single body governed by twenty-four feoffees.

The adaptations made to the building during the 1650s proved sufficient to serve the purposes of the school for a considerable period, though a number of alterations and modifications were made to the library presses, or book cases, during the eighteenth century. These were a result of two distinct trends, firstly the need to create more space, and secondly the abandonment of the practice of chaining the books, which occurred in the mid-eighteenth century and was accompanied by the introduction of an alternative security measure, gates between the presses, still in use today. The shelves were raised at this time, and again by an additional three feet in the late-eighteenth century. Since that time the library has expanded into some of the lower cloistral rooms, but the main ranges remain more or less as they were at the close of the eighteenth century, incorporating the original presses of the mid 1650s made by Martinscrofte (Fig. 60).

The minute books give no indication of substantial alterations and repairs to the building until the nineteenth century (see Appendix 4). The work undertaken then was prompted by two main factors, the deterioration of the fabric and admission of greater numbers of boys. The investments made by the feoffees enabled them to increase numbers from the original forty to around 100 by the 1870s. Initially extra space would have been made by taking back parts of the building previously rented out, for example they were moved from dormitories in the lower cloistral rooms to the upper part of the east range, now used by the school library, at some point in the late eighteenth or early nineteenth century.

60. Library south range, known as the Mary Chapel. The eighteenth century gates between the book cases were introduced when chaining of the books was discontinued

efficacissimo. adeo q: aq̄ detinata p[er]ill[am] eorum
petiit. Ut aūt potasset ex ea rex: festine morti succu
buit. & p[ost] illum homines ū nūli; deinde apta frau
de cumulum t[er]re supposuerunt. Hic q[ue]; fons c[re]
ditur eē ille q[ue]m inuictus martir albanus dū
traheret[ur] ad martirium. sicienti p[ro]p[ter] de t[er]ra arida p[ro]
cliui montis p[ro]duxit. De coronatōe arthuri.

Defuncto aūt rege conuenerunt pontifices
cum clero regni & p[o]p[u]lo ipsumq[ue]; infra cho
ream gigantum more regio humauerunt. E[t]
s[ecun]do dubricius urbis legionum archiep[iscopu]s socia
tis sibi ep[iscop]is & magnatibus: Arthurum filium ei[us] iu
uenē .xv. annorum in rege magnifice erexerunt. Erat
enī inaudite uirtutis atq[ue]; largitatis. Que tantam
gratiam p[re]buit ut a cunctis & ab hostibus amaretur.
Confluebat aūt ad eum tanta militum fortitu
do tantaq[ue]; militantium multitudo: q[uod] sufficient
q[ui]b[us] ille ministraret stipendia distribuenda n[on] h[ab]ēt.
Inuitauerant g[er]e eo t[em]p[o]r[e] saxones contribules suos ex g[er]
mannia & duce colgrino subiugauerant s[ibi] totam

Conclusion

Humphrey Chetham's charity proved to be one of the most munificent and enduring educational charities of seventeenth century Lancashire which had the incidental effect of preserving one of the region's most important medieval buildings. The precincts of the building represent the only extensive relatively untouched ancient site in Manchester city centre, where remains of Norman and possibly Saxon date are probably preserved. The combination of the fifteenth-century buildings and the wealth of seventeenth-century furnishings and fittings is of immeasurable value. The library with original furnishings is nationally important. Other seventeenth- and eighteenth-century fixtures and fittings, the range of furniture made for the hospital, the panelling, doors and door fittings, the decorative plasterwork of the Audit Room and the tympanum in the Reading Room represent an ensemble unique in the Manchester area. Those features mentioned in the building accounts, moreover, can be dated accurately. Had the building not been taken over by the Chetham charity, there can be little doubt that it would only have survived, if at all, in a greatly altered state.

This study represents only one strand within a much wider story, and no attempt has been made to chart the history of the institution in a broader sense. The records held by the library have been the principal source for the building history, and they also give fascinating glimpses into everyday life at the school and library, while lantern slides and photographs provide a visual record from the late nineteenth century (Fig. 62). The children, who were recruited from local parishes with which Chetham had connections, had to be between six and ten years old and from 'honest industrious' families. A typical case might involve the son of a widow, or of parents of small means with a large family to support. Illegitimate children were specifically excluded. The minutes record more than one case of a child being returned because he was found to be born out of wedlock. Other entries flesh out the bones of the dry records. The feoffees are constantly busy with running the institution and administering the

61. Detail from the *Flores Historiarum* by Matthew Paris showing the coronation of King Arthur

property from which it derived income. Arrangements for admission of the boys and their dispatch to an apprenticeship had to be made, and there were continual concerns about their health and welfare. In 1689 we learn of the successful termination of the apprenticeship of Nicholas Clegg, probably to an instrument or clock maker. In 1695 he showed his gratitude through the gift of a delightful tall-case clock and barometer, which still stands in the library reading room. Runaways are dealt with, including boys who managed to get as far as Ashbourne in Derbyshire. A boy ill-treated as an apprentice has his case taken up. Sadder stories appear, of those who succumb to illness, and of the poor little boy sent home for persistent bed-wetting. We learn of the librarian dismissed after his wife was caught selling library property to Manchester booksellers, and the House Governor forced to retire through deafness. A Chetham's boy is the hero of Mrs Linnaeus Banks' novel *The*

62. Pancake Day in the kitchen, 1923

Manchester Man of 1876, which paints a vivid picture of the school and its neighbourhood, but the history of the school and its pupils has been a neglected area, and the records held by the library have the potential for the construction of an important social study.

An extended account of the library and its exceptional holdings would represent another important element of the overall picture. Of more than 100,000 printed books in the collection, 60,000 were published before 1851, including many sixteenth- and seventeenth-century works. There is a fifteenth-century collection of astrological writings, and the jewel in the crown of the medieval manuscripts is the *Flores Historiarum* of Matthew Paris (Fig. 61), written at St Albans and Westminster in the thirteenth and fourteenth centuries. Other items include books of hours, medical manuscripts and early English poetry. A late fifteenth-century manuscript, bound in red goatskin tooled in gold, is from the library of Matthias Corvinus, King of Hungary. More recent works are contained in the Halliwell-Phillipps collection of more than 3,000 broadsides, proclamations and poems, while modern manuscripts include works by Robert Southey and accounts relating to Horace Walpole's expenditure on his house at Strawberry Hill. From the mid-nineteenth century the library started to focus on the north west of England, and it now has one of the largest collections of books, pamphlets and archives relating to the history and topography of the Manchester area, including early newspapers, maps, prints and glass slides.

In a study of this sort it is hardly surprising that as many questions are raised as are answered. The details of the initial building phases, as well as the original function and access arrangements for some of the rooms, are far from clear. The sequence and extent of significant improvements made before the seventeenth century remain obscure, and it is not known who carried them out. The lack of documentary evidence for this earlier period means that some of the questions may never be answered, however the relative abundance of seventeenth century documentation means that there is the possibility of our knowledge about the library and hospital conversion being refined. Chetham's was the subject of more research during the nineteenth century than the twentieth, so re-evaluation in the twenty-first century is perhaps timely, and will, it is hoped, be continued.

Overleaf: 63. Robert Whitworth, The South West Prospect of Manchester and Salford. Hand-coloured engraving, 1734

The South West Prospect
1. Trinity Church Salford.
2. Mr. Miles Nields House.
3. The College
4. Christ Church.
5. The Bridge & Dungeon.
6. The Spaw House.
7. Mr. Moss's Wharf for Boats &c.
8. The Rock House.
9. The 7 Houses in Parsonage.
10. The late Mr. Houghton's Summer House.
11. Mr. Wilsons Cupola.
12. The Exchange.
To the Honourable Ann
Mannor of MANCHESTER.
Her Ladyships

anchester and Salford
Dowager Bland Lady of the
most Humbly Inscribed by
Robert Whitworth
13 Mr. Marsdens Cupola.
14 Mr. Wilkinsons Garden.
15 Mr. Butterworths Cupola
16. St. Anne's Church.
17 Dole Field.
18. The late Mr. Nicholsons
19 Mr. Browns great House.
20 Mr. Sedgwicks Garden &c.
23 Mr. Hawkswells Building.
24 Mr. Pinkethman's his Building.
25 The River Irwell.

APPENDIX ONE

Notes on Colleges of Priests in England and an Architectural Parallel

The secular college of priests is a relatively rare building type, and those which have survived are generally in a greatly altered or fragmentary state. Despite the significance of the Manchester example it has not hitherto been the subject of detailed analysis. An excellent nineteenth-century study by Henry Taylor offers the best description and comparative analysis, with much of value for modern readers.[109] The most recent study, by Anthony Emery, was undertaken as part of a wider survey and describes Chetham's as 'the most complete late-medieval residential complex to survive in the north-west' which 'retains its original plan and character to an unparalleled extent'.[110]

A comparative study of colleges of priests has yet to be undertaken, and the wide variation of the dates and sizes of the establishments, combined with the incomplete state of most, and the lack of archaeological information, means that generalisations cannot easily be made about their architecture and planning. W. A. Pantin lists colleges at Arundel in Sussex; Higham Ferrers, Northamptonshire; Kings Lynn, Norfolk; Maidstone, Kent; Mettingham, Suffolk; Windsor and Wingfield, Suffolk, but his detailed studies were mainly confined to small chantry priests' houses.[111] The college building was attached to the church at Higham Ferrers, and a fourteenth-century college at Cobham in Kent was partially converted into almshouses in the late sixteenth century. The Maidstone example, which dates from the late fourteenth century, is relatively well preserved, though not complete, and it takes a different form from Manchester, with a gate tower, master's house and master's tower.

At Manchester the cloistered accommodation for college members is of particular interest. The rooms vary slightly in size, but most are around sixteen- to seventeen-feet square, giving around 250–80 square feet per room. Exactly how the accommodation was apportioned must be a matter for speculation; if it is assumed that the fellows had a two-room set each and were not obliged to 'chum' together, the rooms compare very favourably with other establishments of this type, with the fellows having between 500–60 square feet of space each. W. A. Pantin's comparative analysis[112] shows that this is predictably far more generous than the modest chantry priest's houses he was concerned with, but it is also more spacious than the domestic lodgings at Dartington Hall, Devon, and Haddon Hall, Derbyshire, for example. It even compares well with the typical accommodation of the Vicars Choral at Lincoln and Wells who had 540 square feet and 520 square feet each respectively.[113] As well as the two-room sets there is the suite of two rooms and a closet above the pantry and buttery, and the two rooms sharing a common stair in the range east of the kitchen, as well as much additional room in that range; ample provision for the four clerks and six choristers with room to spare in the gatehouses for guests. Alternatively if all the college members were housed in the cloistral ranges, a possible arrangement could involve fellows and clerks having one room each (twelve rooms in all) and the six choristers chumming two or three per room. There would still be plenty

64. Wenlock Priory, the cloister range. Country Life Picture Library

of space, at least sixteen rooms, even if we take all or part of the accommodation in the south range out of the equation.

Monastic cloisters are the obvious precedent for the arrangement, but these were not usually two-storeyed. Secular lodgings on two floors usually had internal or external access by individual staircases, as at Dartington Hall and many Oxford and Cambridge colleges.[114] There are comparisons, however, with the late fifteenth-century prior's lodgings at Wenlock Priory, also of two storeys but with only one range (Fig. 64). This has bays divided by buttresses, but with continuous ranges of lights on both floors, and walkways or galleries on two levels giving access to infirmary rooms and the prior's apartment. Christopher Hussey, writing on the Wenlock example, suggests analogies with late medieval French architecture and says: 'These superposed access galleries are the only completely surviving English example in masonry of a medieval planning innovation that nevertheless was rarely adopted in monastic architecture and became typical of the timber-framed courtyards of inns'.[115] The Manchester college cloisters are an antecedent to Wenlock, though it seems that Hussey did not know them.

APPENDIX TWO

Notes on the Structure of the Roof

The roof belongs to a family more usually associated with the box-framed tradition of the south of England, as opposed to cruck-framed tradition of the north-west. It is a type of crown-post roof, with arch-braced tie-beams and a collar-purlin (Fig. 65), but it differs from the usual form in that the crown post has been reduced to the merest stub which is concealed by the arched braces attaching the collar purlin to the tie beam. Common rafter trusses have collars and diagonal braces. The arch braces and collar purlins are deeply moulded

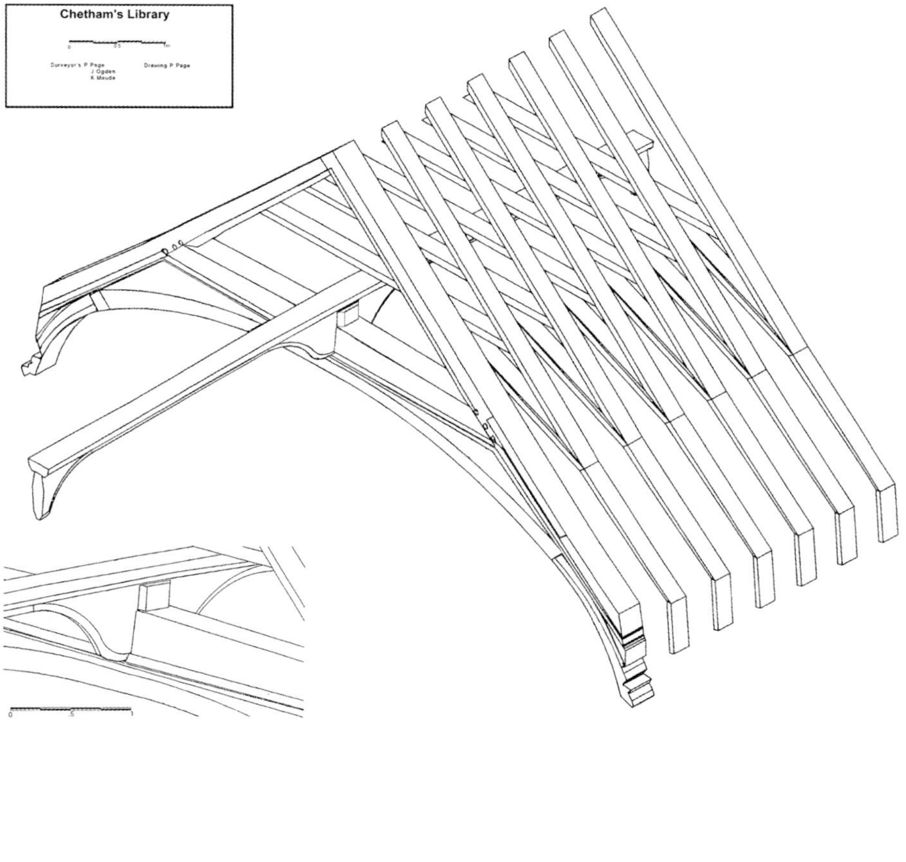

65. Diagram of roof structure by Paul Page and Keith Maude

and where they have not been hacked off the feet of the principals extend below the wall plate. In the hall the only unmutilated examples rise from foliated stone corbels, while in the south part of the library a plain stone corbel survives. A small group of crown post roofs has been identified in the north-west and west of England, though the Chetham's roof seems to be without direct parallels. Lancashire examples include a roof section at Smithill's Hall, Bolton; a roof at Morleys Hall, Leigh; trusses in the east wing of Ordsall Hall, Salford dated to 1360; and an early fifteenth-century roof in St Wilfrid's Church, Ribchester.[116]

The condition of the roof structure is generally good and principal trusses appear to be substantially original. In fact there is no evidence for wholesale replacement of any of the principal roof timbers except those altered, probably in the early eighteenth century, to insert a bellcote, and in the part of the roof above the pantry and buttery damaged in the Second World War. This tends to belie the seventeenth century description of the building which states: 'some of the roof is blown of . . . & the timbers being rotted for [lack] of slate'.[117] Though this could have been a reference to the condition of ancillary buildings since demolished.

APPENDIX THREE

The Dendrochronological Survey

A dendrochronological survey of parts of the building complex was undertaken by Ian Tyers of the Sheffield Dendrochronology Laboratory for English Heritage in 2001. Surveys of this type compare growth rings in samples of timber with one another and with sequences built up from dated timbers elsewhere in the region. The growth rate of the tree is reflected in the rings which are affected by climatic and other conditions leading to the production of identifiable patterns which affect trees across a wide area. It is therefore possible to compare ring sequences obtained from different sources and match them with sequences for which dates are known.

Timbers from the hall and cloistral ranges were sampled and forty-seven cores obtained. It was not possible to obtain samples which included bark edges except in one case, in a timber from the north cloister walkway, which was felled in the spring of 1429. The absence of bark edges meant that it was not possible to arrive at a precise date for any other timbers, however one from the south cloister range was tentatively dated to 1424. The absence of bark edges is an indication of the high level of finish of the timbers, which is consistent with the high status of the college building. The warping of the timbers show that they were used while green, which suggests that felling dates are likely to be coterminous with construction dates, and the results indicated dates for the second quarter of the fifteenth century for most of the timbers sampled. There was a high rate of correlation between samples from different parts of the building which exhibited very similar growth patterns, suggesting the timbers may have been obtained from the same source.

Two samples from the north cloister walkway immediately adjacent to the hall fell into a different category and were dated to the late sixteenth or early seventeenth century. An undated timber from the west side of the hall exhibited similarities in colour and growth rates. These results suggest that this part of the building was modified or repaired during this period, possibly in connection with insertion of a chimney into the hall.

Two shutters which fit the lower cloister windows were also examined, and dated to the late seventeenth or early eighteenth century, suggesting that they were made during or soon after the conversion of the building for Chetham's charity.

A full account of the sampling, including a summary of the methodology and working practices used, was published by English Heritage in 2002,[118] the contents of which form the basis for this note.

APPENDIX FOUR

Nineteenth-Century Restoration, Alteration and New Buildings

Our understanding of how nineteenth-century restorations affected the building is helped by a set of plans, measured drawings and perspectives by John Palmer,[119] the earliest reliable and comprehensive record of the appearance and layout of the building to be identified. Some are dated 1815, and they were probably all made at the same time. Palmer was an architect and antiquarian who may have made the drawings simply for his own interest, or perhaps in anticipation of Samuel Hibbert-Ware's *History of the Foundations in Manchester*, published in 1830, or W. R. Whatton's *A History of Chetham's College and Library* of 1833 which includes engravings made from some of the drawings.

EARLY TO MID NINETEENTH CENTURY

The condition of the building had started to give cause for concern by the beginning of the nineteenth century. In the minutes of the 5th October 1801 the feoffees decided to arrange 'an inspection of the state of repair of the hospital on the northerly side as are immediately wanted and give such order for proceeding as they may think fit'. The gatehouse was refronted in 1815, and the feoffees ordered that this work should be done 'keeping in view its architectural principle'.[120]

Other works include the construction of a laundry and a washhouse in the rear courtyard, approved during the 1820s. In 1841 John Buxton, a builder and timber merchant of Hulme, Manchester, was paid £200 for alterations and repairs to the building, which included improvements to the schoolroom and dormitories. Two years later it was decided to admit more boys and provide additional accommodation for them, which seems to have been completed in 1844–5. Rather surprisingly the relatively new washroom and laundry were swept away for this extension, however its position behind the dormitory block meant that it did not intrude greatly upon the existing building or encroach into the yard.

The *Builder* reported that George Shaw of Saddleworth was working on the building in 1847,[121] though his name is not mentioned in the minute books. Shaw designed several churches in the Manchester area and was a keen antiquarian who had a workshop producing church fittings and domestic furniture in medieval style. Main responsibility for the repairs, however, can be credited to the talented Manchester architect J.E. Gregan (1813–55) and it was probably he who designed the 1844 building which exhibits similarities in detail to the restoration work. An article on Chetham's he wrote in 1851[122] shows that he had made a study of its history and fabric of the building.

There can be no doubt that the crumbling outer walls would have been in urgent need of attention by this time; even those parts replaced or rebuilt in the 1650s would have been ravaged by the effects of the weather and industrial pollution. Summary accounts in the minute books show that almost £8,000 was spent on repairs and new building between 1844 and 1854, with costs peaking in the years 1851–4, after which time the annual repair bill falls to between £100 and £300. Gregan's name is not mentioned until 1851, when the minutes record on 30 July:

> Resolved that the repairs and alterations in the college building referred to in the estimates of Mr Ibbetson and other plans prepared by Mr Gregan laid before the meeting be considered.

He was probably involved before, but the exact way in which the campaign of repair was planned and carried out is obscure. The minutes of 2 April 1852 authorise the local committee to:

> proceed with the restoration of the outside of the hospital extending from the porch recently restored to the eastern gateway. Cost (including architect's commission) £494 10*s.* 6*d.*

Palmer's drawings (Figs. 17 and 66) show that Gregan regularised the exterior appearance of the building, particularly in the east wing, and in some places new openings were introduced. In Palmer's time the ground floor windows of the east range were simple flat-headed mullions without labels, rather like some of the windows surviving in the north elevation. More elaborate windows with cusping and labels were introduced, and although most of the upper windows retained the original appearance, they seem to have been enlarged and some have obviously been repositioned. The greatest changes were made in the angled range beside the gatehouse and the two bays of the range beside it where signs of considerable alteration or rebuilding are shown by Palmer. These rooms had been let out in the 1650s, so the alterations may relate to this or an earlier period, or possibly to a time in the late part of that century when they were taken back by the school. Gregan reinstated the double string course which formerly petered out here, and mismatching windows were replaced with copies of medieval windows. A new doorway was introduced to replace an opening at the junction of the angled range, and the windows there, which are shown by Palmer and others as three light mullioned windows, rather like those of the library, were replaced with windows with cusping and labels.

The gable of the warden's lodgings was remodelled losing the kneelers and pinnacles. Even more radical were the alterations to the porch, which seems to have been almost completely rebuilt. The bay to the warden's lodgings was taken as a model, and a nicely balanced composition achieved, unfortunately at the cost of our full understanding of this part of the building. As we have seen the porch is shown in the late eighteenth and early nineteenth centuries with a flat roof and parapet instead of the present gable and niche. It was rebuilt forward of the original line, blocking one of the kitchen windows.

66. East range of the building drawn by John Palmer, *c.* 1815. Greater Manchester County Record Office

The southern boundary of the site was extended to its present line in 1869, when land was bought from Manchester Corporation and the wall and railings erected to the designs of the City Surveyor J. Lynde. The whole of this area had become an appalling slum in the nineteenth century and Lynde's new wall had a ditch running along its inner side to prevent the boys communicating with passers-by.

The next major phase of alteration took place during the 1870s when the feoffees appointed Alfred Waterhouse to design a new schoolroom and carry out alterations to the library. He was instructed to prepare plans and drawing of the building and these were placed in the Library.[123] The new schoolroom was finally erected after many delays in 1876–7. It is a modest, nicely detailed building looking a little like a chapel or Sunday school. The detailing is Perpendicular but the motifs of the main building have not been slavishly adopted. Red sandstone was used and roof timbers exposed. It is notable that some of the feoffees were anxious to ensure that it should be built in stone, not brick,[124] presumably so that it would harmonise with the existing building.

67. Cloister courtyard showing the chimney and stair tower before the 1890s restoration

Waterhouse's alterations to the main building were aimed at improving circulation and achieving separation in the school and library, and work was given the go-ahead in 1876. He inserted a staircase into the room at the south-west corner of the cloister, and this became the main entrance to the library, as it is today. The ground floor rooms beneath the library's west range which were made to interconnect and furnished with new windows. Waterhouse had intended to replace the original library bookshelves but we can be grateful that the feoffees resisted this proposal.[125]

The tradition of retaining first-rate architects for works to the building continued when J. Medland & Henry Taylor carried out repairs funded by one of the feoffees, Oliver Heywood, in the late 1880s. Repairs continued in the 1890s when Heywood's brother Charles undertook to pay for the completion of the work following Oliver's death. The architects submitted specifications for three dormer lights in the western corridor of the library,[126] but most of the work took place in the cloister. The relatively sheltered site may have protected it from the worst effects of the weather and aerial pollution, as it seems to have escaped previous restoration. However it is evident that both the stair tower and chimney had become very decayed by the end of the century (Fig. 67). The Taylors rebuilt the chimney and inglenook creating the present fireplace and low seats. The outer walls and roof of the stair tower also received substantial restoration, and attention was given to the cloister windows. It seems likely that it was during this phase of work that the plaster counter ceilings, which concealed most of the roof structure, were removed, and the minutes record removal of those in the dormitories in 1890.[127] Henry Taylor was a noted antiquarian, and author of *The Old Halls of Lancashire and Cheshire* (1884),

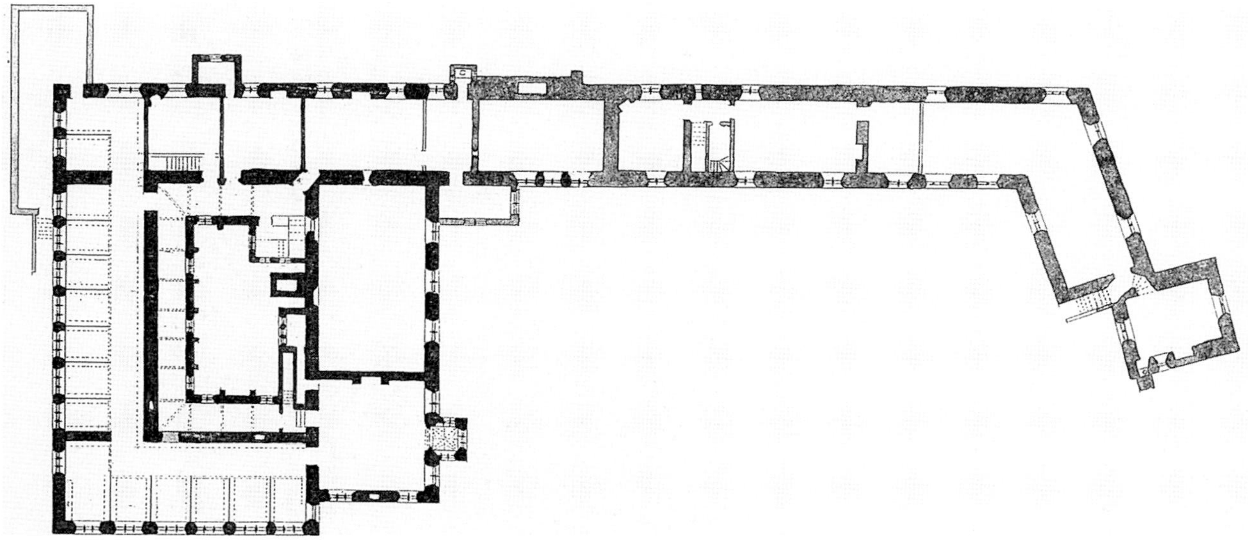

68. Plan by John Palmer *c.* 1815 showing the first floor of the building before alteration by Alfred Waterhouse

which has been noted for its scholarly description of Chetham's. Taylor, in a footnote, states that some of the ceilings were removed shortly after he had completed his account.[128]

OTHER NINETEENTH CENTURY BUILDINGS

The buildings of the Manchester Grammar School along Long Millgate were taken over by Chetham's in 1978. The northernmost, beside the gatehouse, was constructed in 1869–70 by Barker & Ellis of Manchester. The neighbouring building, by another Manchester firm, Mills & Murgatroyd, went up in 1877. The Palatine Buildings on the west side of the site, taken over by Chetham's in 1969, originated as an hotel put up in 1842–3, probably in anticipation of the opening of Victoria Station. The architects were J.P. & I. Holden, and the original proprietor a Mr Gill. The erection of all these buildings feature in the minute books. The building of the hotel, in particular, led to seemingly endless quarrels about the boundary and ancient lights, and it is ironic, considering the protracted nature of the disagreements, that part of the land it stands on was once the property of the hospital, sold off in the 1650s for a house of correction.

APPENDIX FIVE

Building Accounts 1656–8

Transcribed and introduced by Jane Foster, Chetham's Library Archivist

The document was written by one scribe between 25 July 1656 and 10 April 1658. The scribe wrote the document in a clear and well-formed secretary hand, which is riddled with inconsistencies. Spelling, capitalisation and punctuation vary throughout the document, and are dependent upon the idiosyncrasy of the scribe. These inconsistencies have been followed in the transcription, and no attempt has been made to standardise capitalisation and punctuation in the modern form. Abbreviations have been silently extended, while editorial additions to the manuscript text appear in square brackets. Square brackets have also been used where the text is illegible or the supplied extension is doubtful. To help the researcher read the document with ease, the occasional mistaken repetition by the scribe, for example William William Williamson, has been removed.

The accounts are contained in a booklet consisting of 16 pages of strong rag paper measuring approximately 213 × 325 mm. The condition of the outer pages has suffered from the document being stored for many years without any form of cover or binding, but the inside pages are well preserved. In October 1999 the document was sent to Cyril Formby, Chetham's Library Conservator, for intensive cleaning and repair. The document was washed aqueously and with a solution of alcohol to clear away as much dirt as possible. Despite this treatment the first page remains heavily marked and a considerable amount of text is faded or obscured by the deeply ingrained dirt. The cleaning was followed by deacidification using calcium hydroxide. A small portion of the top of the two outer leaves had been torn away many years ago, fortunately without removing any of the text. The conservator repaired the damage using handmade paper and concluded the conservation by binding the document. It is now bound into boards made of archival millboard, with a parchment spine reinforced with unbleached cotton to ensure its durability.

A full transcription of the document was made by the antiquarian John Eglington Bailey in the nineteenth century. Bailey's transcription is full of corrections and additions. An index of personal names and parts of the building, such as the Great Chamber and the Gallery, which appears at the beginning of the transcription, is worthy of note. So too are the occasional comments written in pencil, which appear throughout Bailey's text. These pencil notes, in the hand of John Owen, provide genealogical details about the workmen, for example 'Hercule Chadwick christens children in 1637 & 1644'.

		£	*s.*	*d.*
f. 1	Paid to John Wollen the 25th of July 1656 for twoe dozen of Clasps for bookes as may appeare by his note	00	01	04
	paid to John Rylands the 25th of July 1656 for paintinge [stuffe] for the Library, as may appeare by his note	00	06	04
	paid to John Rylandes the same tyme for [400^{li}] of double [Spike]	00	03	04
	paid to William Williamson the 25th of July 1656 for Eleven foote and [½] of [new] glasse at 4*d.* ½ per foote and for 186 quarrelles of glasse and for sodering and pininge old glasse	01	01	00
	paid to Hercules the Carpenter the 25th of July 1656 for 4 dayes worke of one man at 1*s.* per diem	00	04	00
	paid to Raphe Arderne the 26 of July 1656 for six [meate] piggons for the use of the hospitall	00	01	06
	paid the 26 July 1656 for 2 butter potts	00	00	10
	paid more the same tyme for other 2 pottes	00	00	02
	paid to Henry Walker the 26th of July 1656 for a weekes worke of twoe men and for one dayes worke of one man pointinge the Library	00	13	00
	paid the 28th of July 1656 to James Barrett for twoe double railes for the use of the Hospitall	00	02	06
	paid to John Rylands 28th of July 1656 for one ounce of Indigo	00	[0]	04
	paid to John Freeman the 28th of July 1656 for a bedcoard for the use of the Hospitall	00	01	02
	paid to Francis Cleaton the 31° of July 1656 for 6 loades of Lyme for the use of the Hospitall	00	10	00
	paid to John Rylands the 31° of July 1656 for 3 pound of varnish for the use of the Library	00	02	06
	paid to John C[u]rtis the 31° July 1656 for makeinge 2 boulsters and soweinge three blankettes for the use of the Hospitall	00	00	06
	paid the 31° July 1656 for twoe drinking glasses and 3 wyne glasses	00	01	10
	paid to Edward Miller the 2° of August 1656 for a S[comer] for the use of the Hospitall	00	02	02
	paid to Thurstan Digle the 2° of August 1656 for 17^{li} ½ weight of great nailes for the Library doore, for a fire shovell for the Hospitall, for a Smoothinge Iron and a litle locke as may appeare by his note	00	15	04
	[TOTAL:]	04	07	10

		£	s.	d.
f. 1v	Paid to William Sorro[cold] the 2° of August 1656 for 7 foote of glasse at *4d.* ½ per foote for the use of the Hospitall	00	02	07
	paid to him the same tyme for 20 quarrells	00	01	02
	paid to him the same tyme for leading, sodering and bandinge of Casementes in the Hospitall	00	01	07
	paid to John Chetam the 2° of August 1656 for carriage of one loade of flaggs from Roachdale for the use of the Hospitall	00	06	00
	paid to Richard Martinscroft the Joyner the 2° of August 1656 for 4 dayes worke & ½ of himselfe and 4 dayes worke & ½ of his sonn either of them at 1*s.* 2*d.* per diem	00	10	06
	paid to Richard Martinscroft the same tyme for 4 dayes worke & ½ of his man at 1*s.* per diem	00	04	06
	paid Hercules Chadwicke the Carpenter 2° August 1656 for 5 dayes worke of one man at 1*s.* per diem	00	05	00
	paid to Jeremy Woosencroft the 2° of August 1656 for a new locke and a key and for mending 3 lockes for the use of the Hospitall	00	07	00
	paid Henry Walker the Whiter 2° of August 1656 for 5 dayes worke of 2 men at 1*s.* a peece per diem	00	10	00
	paid to Humphry Peacocke 2° of August 1656 for Cooper worke for the use of the Hospitall	00	04	06
	paid the 2° of August 1656 for 2 earthen pottes for the use of the Hospitall	00	01	02
	paid the 2° of August 1656 for a Temm-sive & for spigottes and focettes	00	00	04
	paid John Rylands the 4th of August 1656 for 200 of double spikes	00	01	08
	paid to Humphry Peacocke the 4th of August 1656 for a hogg-head to keepe washing water in	00	03	09
	paid to Hercules Chadwicke the Carpenter the 5th of August 1656 for a dayes worke of one man	00	01	00
	paid to Kirshall the 5th of August 1656 for dresseinge the houses of office in the Hospitall	00	01	00
	[TOTAL:]	03	01	09
f. 2	Paid to William Pown[all] the 6 of August 1656 for 4 loade of lyme at 1*s.* 6*d.* per loade for the use of the Hospitall	00	06	00
	paid to Robert Kirshall the 8th of August 1656 for 3 loade of lyme for the use of the Hospitall	00	04	06
	paid to John Chetam the 9th of August 1656 for carryinge of one Loade of flaggs from Roachdale	00	06	00
	paid the 9th of August for a vinigar bottell	00	00	04
	paid the 9th of August 1656 to Richard Martinscroft for 3 dayes worke & ½ of himselfe, and 3 dayes worke and ½ of his sonn either of them at 1*s.* 2*d.* per diem, and for 3 dayes worke and an halfe of his man at 1*s.* per diem	00	11	08
	paid the 9th of August 1656 for 9 wooden butter dishes and a pot lidd for the use of the hospitall	00	02	00

		£	*s.*	*d.*
	paid the same tyme for 6 water boules for the boyes to wash in	00	00	10
	paid to Samuell Hollinworth the 11th of August 1656 for one hoope of leather patches for the use of the hospitall	00	01	08
	paid to Samuell Walker the 15th of August 1656 for a locke and a key, and a plate for a deske in the Library	00	02	06
	paid to m^{r} James Lightbowne the 15th of August 1656 for twelve Catachismes bought for the hospitall boyes	00	00	10
	paid to Jonathan Hargreave and John Chetam the 16° of August 1656 for leadinge either of them one loade of flaggs from Roachdale	00	12	00
	paid to Henry Walker the Whiter the 16th of August 1656 for 10 dayes worke of a man in triminge m^{r} Brownes & the Cookes Chamber	00	10	00
	paid to Richard Martinscroft the Joyner the 16° of August 1656 for 4 dayes worke of himselfe and 4 dayes worke of his son either of them at 1*s.* 2*d.* per diem	00	09	04
	paid to Richard Martinscroft the same tyme for 4 dayes worke of his man at 1*s.* per diem	00	04	00
	paid to Jeremy Woosencroft the 18th of August 1656 for a locke and a key for the doore in the upper end in the Library	00	03	00
	[TOTAL:]	03	14	08
f. 2^{v}	Paid to Jeremy Woosencroft the 18th of August 1656 for byndinge a pann for the use of the hospitall	00	03	00
	paid to Lawrance Garner the 18th of August 1656 for 5^{li} of brasse to bee Clasps for bookes	00	06	09
	paid to him the same tyme for 39^{li} and ¼ of pewter for the use of the hospitall at 1*s.* 4*d.* per^{li}	02	12	00
	paid to him the same tyme for a brasse pott of 35^{li} weight at 7*d.* per pound	01	00	05
	paid to him the same tyme as may appeare by his note for a brasse pann of 9^{li} an eleven ounces at 1*s.* 6*d.* per^{li}	00	14	06
	paid to Peter Dickson the 18th of August 1656 for layinge 140 yards of board floores at 4*d.* per yard	02	06	00
	paid to him the same tyme for makeinge a presse for the use of the hospitall	00	07	06
	paid to him the same tyme for makeinge 2 syde posts for a doore, & for hanginge the doore	00	01	00
	paid to William Symon the 19th of August 1656 for makeinge 24^{li} weight of Iron rodds for the Library at 4*d.* per^{li}	00	08	00
	paid to James Greaves the 22° of August 1656 for the Carriage of one loade of flaggs from Roachdale	00	06	00
	paid to John Rylands the 23th of August 1656 in discharge of his note for paintinge stuffe for m^{r} Brownes Chamber	00	08	08
	paid to him more for 3^{li} of Ash Coloure for triminge the Cookes Chamber	00	00	06

		£	s.	d.
	paid to Jeremy Woosencroft the 23th of August 1656 for 45^{li} weight of Iron rodds for the Library at 4*d.* per pound	00	15	00
	paid to him the same tyme for a paire of bands for the doore in the lower end of the Library	00	02	06
	paid to John Chetham the 23th of August 1656 for the Carriage of a Loade of flaggs from Roachdale	00	06	00
	[TOTAL:]	09	17	10
f. 3	Paid to James Greaves the 23th of August 1656, for leadinge one loade of flaggs from Roachdale	00	06	00
	paid to Francis Cleaton the 23th of August 1656 for 4 loade of lyme at 1*s.* 8*d.* per loade	00	06	08
	paid for a wiskett the 23th of August 1656 for the use of the hospitall	00	00	04
	paid the same tyme for a twiggen voyder and a twigen baskett for the use of the hospitall	00	02	04
	paid the 23 of August 1656 to Thurstan Digle for a locke and key for the Library	00	02	08
	paid to him the same tyme for an Iron Chafeing dish for the use of the hospitall	00	01	04
	paid to Richard Martinscroft the Joyner the 23th August 1656 for 3 dayes worke & ½ of himselfe at 1*s.* 2*d.* per diem, and for 3 dayes worke & ½ of his man at 1*s.* per diem	00	07	07
	paid the same tyme to George Martinscroft for a weekes worke of himselfe at 1*s.* 2*d.* per diem	00	07	00
	paid the 23 August 1656 for an earthen pott	00	00	03
	paid Edward Platt the Mason the 23th of August 1656 for ten Loade of stone for the stayres to the Library, 3 loade whereof were at 2*s.* per loade and 7 loade at 1*s.* per loade	00	13	00
	paid to him the same tyme for the chimney stones in the hall	00	05	00
	paid to him more the same tyme for leadeinge of the said ten loade of stone at 1*s.* 2*d.* per load	00	11	08
	paid the 25th of August 1656 for twoe Rowlinge pinns and a battrell	00	01	00
	paid the 26 of August 1656 for an earthen pott	00	00	02
	paid to Richard Martinscroft the Joyner the 30th of August 1656 for one day worke of himselfe at 1*s.* 2*d.* per diem, & for 3 dayes worke of his sonn at 1*s.* 2*d.* per diem, and for one day worke of his man at 1*s.* per diem	00	05	08
	paid to James Greeves the 30th of August 1656 for the carriage of one loade of flaggs from Roachdale	00	06	00
	paid to John Piersevall the 1° of September 1656 for a fire Iron for m^{r} Browne his Chamber weighinge 21^{li} and an other fire Iron for the use of the hospitall weighinge 65^{li} both of them at 3*d.* 3 farthinges a pound	01	07	00
	[TOTAL:]	05	03	08

		£	*s.*	*d.*
f. 3^{v}	Paid to George Walker the 2° of September 1656 for mendinge the boyes Cloathes	00	00	06
	paid to John Chetham the 3° of September 1656 for carriage of one Loade of Flaggs from Roachdale	00	06	00
	paid to Thomas Greaves the fourth of September 1656 for the Carriage of one Load of flaggs from Roachdale	00	06	00
	paid to John Nuttall the 6th of September 1656 for the Carriage of one loade of flaggs from Roachdale	00	06	00
	paid to Robert Dickson the 6th of September 1656 for the Carriage of one loade of flaggs from Roachdale	00	06	00
	paid to Raphe Seddon the 6th of September 1656 for the Carriage of one Loade of flaggs from Roachdale	00	06	00
	paid to Thomas Hoult the 6th of September 1656 for the Carriage of one loade of flaggs from Roachdale	00	06	00
	paid to James Greaves the 6th of September 1656 for the Carriage of one loade of flaggs from Roachdale	00	06	00
	paid to Richard Martinscroft the Joyner the 6th of September 1656 for 2 dayes worke and ½ of himselfe at 1*s.* 2*d.* per diem, & for a weekes worke of his sonn at 1*s.* 2*d.* per diem, and for 2 dayes worke of his man at 1*s.* per diem	00	11	11
	paid the sixt day of September 1656 for glue and nailes	00	00	04
	paid to Jeremiah Woosencroft the sixt day of September 1656 for 60 pound & ¾ of Iron rodds for the Librarie at 4*d.* per^{li}	01	00	00
	paid to him the same tyme for foure hookes and stables, for the booke frame in m^{r} Browns Chamber	00	00	04
	[TOTAL:]	03	15	01
f. 4	Paid to Jeremie Woosencroft the 6th of September 1656 for a longe Iron pinn & a stable for the use of the Library	00	00	08
	paid to William Hyde the 6th of September 1656 for 2 Eshons and a Runge	00	06	08
	paid the same day for 2 earthen pottes	00	00	03
	paid Edward Sandiford the 6th of September 1656 for six Towell pinns	00	04	00
	paid the 12th of September 1656 for foure measures to measure Corne	00	03	00
	paid 12th of September 1656 to Richard Martinscroft the Joyner for 4 dayes worke of himselfe at 1*s.* 2*d.* per diem & for 4 dayes worke of his man at 1*s.* per diem	00	08	08
	paid to John Nuttall and James Seddon the 13th of September 1656 for the Carriage of twoe loade of flaggs from Roachdale	00	12	00
	paid the 16th of September 1656 to Randall Kenerley for the Carriage of 2 Mapps from London	00	02	06
	paid to George Farmarie the 16th of September 1656 for a plate for a deske in the Library	00	01	06
	paid to Ann Rawstorne the 16th of September 1656 for Ale had for Richard Martinscroft	00	02	00
	paid the 16th September 1656 for a Lanterne	00	01	00

	£	s.	d.
paid the 18th of September 1656 for byndinge 4 Corne measures for the use of the hospitall	00	03	00
paid Richard Martinscroft the Joyner the 18th of September 1656, for 4 dayes worke of himselfe at 1*s*. 2*d*. per diem, and for 3 dayes worke of his sonn at 1*s*. 2*d*. per diem, and for 4 dayes worke of his man at 1*s*. per diem	00	12	02
paid widowe Seddon the 19th of September 1656 for keepeinge her sonn a moneth beinge sicke	00	06	08
paid to Jeremy Woosencroft the 19th of September 1656 for 34li ½ of Iron rodds for the Library at 4*d*. per pound	00	11	06
paid to him the same tyme for a longe Iron pinn for the use of the Library & for 2 lockes for the Library	00	05	04
paid to Henry Walker the 19th of September 1656 for one day worke of one man in shooting and some other worke	00	01	00
[TOTAL:]	04	01	11

f. 4v

	£	s.	d.
Paid the 19th of September 1656 for earthen pottes	00	01	06
paid or given the workemen in drinke the 22th day of September 1656	00	00	04
paid to John Cheetham the 24th of September 1656 for the Carriage of one Loade of flaggs from Roachdale	00	06	00
paid to John Cheetham the 27th of September 1656 for leadinge of one loade of flaggs from Roachdale	00	06	00
paid to William Hyde the 27th of September 1656 for a Runge and twoe other vessells for the use of the hospitall	00	07	00
paid the 27th of September 1656 for 8 yards of Twill for a Chaffebedd for the use of the hospitall	00	04	00
paid Edward Platt the Mason the 27th of September 1656 for 8 dayes worke of himselfe at 1*s*. 4*d*. per diem and for 9 dayes worke of one man at 1*s*. 2*d*. per diem and for 9 dayes worke of another man at 1*s*. per diem, and for 5 dayes worke of another man at 1*s*. per diem for the Library staires	01	15	02
paid to William Bardsley the 27th of September 1656 for a Table for mr Brownes Chamber	00	12	00
paid or given to the workmen in drinke 2° October 1656	00	00	03
paid to Thomas Irlam the 4th of October 1656 for leadeinge twoe loade of Sand from Broughton foard	00	01	08
paid to Jeremy Woosencroft the fourth of October 1656 for a locke for the backe doore in the Library and for six spradds and a plate for the backe doore in the hall	00	03	03
paid to Raphe Smith the Breeke layer the 8th of October 1656 for makeinge an hobb and settinge a fire Iron in mr Browns Chamber	00	01	00
paid Edmund Cleaton the 9th of October 1656 for three Loades of Lyme at one shilling eight pence the loade	00	05	00
[TOTAL:]	04	03	02

		£	s.	d.
f. 5	Paid to Edward Platt the 11th of October 1656 for one weekes worke of himselfe at 1*s.* 4*d.* per diem, and a weekes worke of one man at 1*s.* 2*d.* per diem, and for 5 dayes of another man at 1*s.* per diem and for another 3 dayes worke at 1*s.* per diem for the Library staires	01	03	00
	paid more to Edward Platt the 11th of October 1656 for 4 dayes worke of himselfe at 1*s.* 4*d.* per diem, and for 2 dayes worke of one man at 1*s.* 2*d.* and for 2 dayes worke of twoe men either of them at 1*s.* a peece per diem, and for another 2 dayes worke at 1*s.* per diem for the Library staires	00	13	08
	paid to Jeremie Woosencroft the 11th of October 1656 for 5 Lockes and plates for the Library	00	12	06
	paid to Edmund Cleaton the 14th of October 1656 for 7 loade of Lyme at 1*s.* 8*d.* per loade	00	11	08
	paid to Edward Platt the Mason the 14th of October 1656 for one dayes worke of himselfe at 1*s.* 4*d.* per diem, and for one dayes worke of one man at 1*s.* 2*d.* per diem and for one dayes worke of 3 men each of them at 1*s.* a peece per diem for the Library staires	00	05	06
	paid the 15th of October 1656 for a wiskett for the use of the hospitall	00	00	04
	paid to Henry Pierson the 18th of October 1656 for 40 dozen yardes of Cheanes for the Library at 4*s.* per dozen as may appeare by his note	08	00	00
	paid the 18th of October 1656, to Thomas Hoult for the Carriage of one Loade of flaggs from Rachdale	00	06	00
	paid to John Chetham the 18th of October 1656 for the Carriage of one loade of Flaggs from Roachdale	00	06	00
	paid to Richard Martinscroft the Joyner the 18th of October 1656 for a weekes worke of himself in Cheaneinge the bookes in the Library	00	07	00
	paid to Francis Cleaton the 21th of October 1656 for 2 loade of Lyme for the use of the hospitall	00	03	04
	[TOTAL:]	12	09	00
f. 5v	Paid to Francis Cleaton the 23th of October 1656 for twoe loade of Lyme for the use of the hospitall	00	03	00
	paid to James Greaves the 25th of October 1656 for leadeinge of one loade of Flaggs from Rachdale for the use of the hospitall	00	06	00
	paid to Francis Cleaton the 25th of October 1656 for 2 loade of Lyme for the use of the hospitall	00	03	04
	paid to Jeremy Woosencroft the 25th of October 1656 for 52li weight of Iron Rodds for the Library at 4*d.* perli	00	17	04
	paid to him the same tyme for a stable for the Library	00	00	04
	paid to him the same tyme for mendinge the handle of the well	00	00	04
	paid to Richard Martinscroft the Joyner the 25th of October 1656 for a weekes worke of himselfe at 1*s.* 2*d.* per diem in Cheaneinge the bookes	00	07	00

		£	*s.*	*d.*
	paid the 29th of October 1656 for 2 Mapps for the washinge of the Library floore	00	02	00
	paid the 31° of October 1656 to Francis Cleaton for 2 loade of Lyme for the use of the hospitall	00	03	04
	paid to Henry Walker the 1° of November 1656 for one day worke of himselfe and one day worke of his man in whiteing & shooteinge	00	02	00
	paid to him the same tyme for varnish	00	00	06
	paid to William Williamson the 3° November 1656 for 2 foote & ½ of glasse for the use of the hospitall	00	01	00
	paid the 3° of November 1656 for Leather patches for the use of the hospitall	00	00	06
	paid to a woman the 6° of November 1656 for helpeinge to wash the Library floore	00	00	06
	[TOTAL:]	02	07	02
f. 6	Paid to John Whitehead the 9th November 1656 for makeinge 21 dozen of Clasps for books in the Library	00	10	06
	paid to John Freeman the 12th of November 1656 for a Cord to hange Cloathes upon	00	01	02
	paid to Jeremy Woosencroft the 15th of November 1656 for 7 lockes for the Library at 2*s.* 6*d.* per locke	00	17	06
	paid to Richard Martinscroft the Joyner the 15th of November 1656 for a weekes worke of himselfe at 1*s.* 2*d.* per diem	00	07	00
	paid to William Symond the 15th of November 1656 for makeinge 32 dozen of Clasps at 2*d.* ½ per dozen	00	06	08
	paid to him the same tyme for 1li and ¼ of brasse at 1*s.* perli and for makeinge it into Nyne dozen of Clasps for the bookes in the Library	00	03	01
	paid to William Hyde the 15th of November 1656 for 2 Kimnelles to set under the beere barrelles	00	02	08
	paid to James Barrett the 20th of November 1656 for 600 of Sapp-Lattes for the use of the hospitall as may appeare by his note	00	12	04
	paid to him the same tyme for 2 wheele beedes	00	13	04
	paid to him the same tyme for 19 yardes of seeleinge in the hospitall hall at 2*s.* 8*d.* per yard	02	10	08
	paid to him the same tyme for 2 litle tables for the boyes Chambers	00	12	00
	paid to Hercules the Carpenter the 20th of November 1656 for 3 dayes worke of one man	00	03	00
	paid the 21° of November 1656 for a paire of snuffers	00	01	00
	paid to Jeremy Woosencroft the 21° November 1656 for three dozen and an halfe of Sockettes for the Library at foure shillings the dozen	00	14	00
	[TOTAL:]	07	14	11

		£	s.	d.
f. 6v	Paid to the Mason the 21th of November 1656 for layinge a flagg over the washing pann	00	00	08
	paid the same tyme the 21th of November 1656 for some woodden vesselles for the hospitall	00	01	02
	paid to Raphe Wollen the 28th of November 1656 for 9 dozen of Clasps at one tyme and for 14 dozen of Clasps for the Library bookes received the day aforesaid at 5*d.* ½ per dozen	00	10	06
	paid to Raphe Wollen the same tyme for 4li weight of Brasse for Clasps at 1*s.* perli	00	04	00
	paid more the same tyme to Raphe Wollen for 7li ½ of brasse to bee Clasps 1*s.* perli	00	07	06
	paid to Richard Martinscroft the Joyner the 29th of November 1656 for 4 dayes worke & ½ of himselfe at 1*s.* 2*d.* per diem, and for one weekes worke of his sonn at 1*s.* 2*d.* per diem, and for a weekes worke of his man at 1*s.* per diem	00	18	03
	paid to Edward Gryme the 29th of November 1656 for a ladder which was lost in the hospitall worke	00	02	06
	paid to Jeremy Woosencroft the 29th of November 1656 for a Locke and a key for the Closset in the great Chamber in the hospitall	00	03	04
	paid to George Martinscroft the Joyner the 5th of December 1656 for 3 dayes worke of himselfe at 1*s.* 2*d.* per diem, and for 3 dayes worke and a peece of his man at 1*s.* per diem	00	06	10
	paid to Jeremy Woosencroft the 6° of December 1656 for 4 Lockes for the Library, and a hammer for the Library doore	00	10	10
	paid to him the same day for a brundritt for the smoothing Iron	00	00	03
	paid to Jeremy Woosencroft the 10th of December 1656 for 7li weight of Iron rodds for the Library at 4*d.* per pound	00	02	04
	paid to him the same tyme for 2 sockettes for the Library	00	00	08
	[TOTAL:]	03	08	10

f. 7	Paid the 11th of December 1656 for an Iron peele, and a plate to sett before the dreepeinge pann	00	08	00
	paid to George Martinscroft the Joyner the 13th of December 1656 for a weekes worke of himselfe at 1*s.* 2*d.* per diem and for 3 dayes worke and ½ of his man at 1*s.* per diem	00	10	06
	paid to John Hoult the 13th of December 1656 for the Carriage of one Loade of Flaggs from Roachdale	00	06	00
	paid the 13th of December 1656 for a Towell pinn	00	00	08
	paid the 13th of December 1656 for 3 yardes of boulsteringe	00	03	02
	paid the 15th of December 1656 to George Martinscroft the Joyner for one dayes worke of his man	00	01	00
	paid the 19th of December 1656 to Jeffrey Scott for exchange of a pott	00	08	09
	paid to Jeremy Woosencroft the 23th of December 1656 for a broyleing Iron & a grid Iron	00	07	00
	paid the 24th of December 1656 for Ale had for Richard Martinscroft since the sixteenth of September last	00	03	10

	£	s.	d.
paid to Edward Platt the Mason the 25th December 1656 for flagging part of the Hall in the Hospitall being 97 yards at 4*d.* per yard	01	12	00
paid more to him the same day for one day worke of a man	00	01	00
paid more to him the same day for 5 dayes worke of a man in breakeing up the hall floore and Carryinge sand	00	05	00
paid to John Piersevall the 26th of December 1656 for alteringe the fire Iron in the Hall	00	05	06
paid the 26 of December 1656 to the breekelayer for setinge the fire Iron in the Hall	00	01	00
paid to Edward Turner the 26th of December 1656 for removeinge earth and rubbidge	00	01	00
[TOTAL:]	04	14	05

f. 7v

Paid to Gilbert Smith the 1° of January 1656 for nailes for the use of the hospitall	01	14	00
paid the Third of January 1656 for five dozen of Clasps made in Wigan for the Library	00	04	00
paid to Jeremy Woosencroft the 22th of January 1656 for a locke and a key for the great Chamber doore in the hospitall	00	03	04
paid to Willaim Williamson the 23th of January 1656 for 10 foote of glasse and for some odd quarrelles for the use of the hospitall	00	04	00
paid the 24th of January 1656 to Thurstan Digle for a shovell for the use of the Hospitall	00	02	06
[TOTAL:]	02	07	10
Wee have examined this booke and there is disburst in it for the use of the hospitall one hundreth thirtie and six poundes nyne shillings tenn pence, wee say January 30th 1656 seene and allowed by us Henry Wrigley Raphe Worsley	136	09	10
Wee whose names are subscribed doe find under the Treasurers hand mr James Lightbowne, that the whole summe paid to mr Richard Dutton by mr Edmund Chetam, and mr James Lightbowne since the 8th of Aprill 1656 to this 30th of January 1656 is just twoe hundreth Three score and five poundes, wee say	265	00	00
And that mr Richard Duttons disbursementes set downe in this booke is one hundreth & thirtie six pounds nyne shillings tenn pence, And his disbursementes set downe in his weekes bill booke is the sume of one hundreth and thirtie poundes seaven shillings five pence, which together in disbursementes doe make	266	17	03
Soe that at this account made the 30th day of January 1656 there restes due since the last account Thirtie seaven shillings and three pence, and more there did rest due to mr Richard Dutton before the last account Nyne pounds and six pence which being added together there resteth due to mr Richard Dutton this present day Ten pounds seaventeene shillings & Nyne pence, wee say	010	17	09

Examined by us Henry Wrigley Raphe Worsley

		£	*s.*	*d.*
f. 8	Paid the 2° of February 1656 for a paire of bands to bee used in m^{r} Brownes Chamber	00	00	04
	paid the same day to Raphe Wollen for nailes to fix the bookes in the Library as may appeare by his note	00	03	03
	paid the same tyme for a garden rake	00	01	02
	paid the 11th of February 1656 for a plate for the backe doore in the hospitall, and for 3^{li} of leade for sodering the plate into the wall at the backe doore	00	01	02
	paid Edward Platt the Mason the 12th of February 1656 for hewinge the backe doore and for soderinge the plate at the back doore	00	00	06
	paid to Jeremy Woosencroft the 6° of March 1656 for 2 great Iron pinns & for the broken beame in the great parloure in the hospitall	00	06	08
	paid the 6th of March 1656 for 8 loade of sand, & 5 loade of Clay for the use of the Hospitall	00	05	01
	paid the 7th of March 1656 for 10 Yards of Twill for Chaires and stooles at 8*d.* per Yard	00	06	08
	paid the same tyme for 18 Yards of Canves for Chaires and stooles at 6*d.* per Yard	00	09	00
	paid the same tyme for 2 Yards and ¾ of flaxen Cloath for a Table Cloath for the hospitall	00	03	01
	paid to Hercules Chadwicke the Carpenter the 7th of March 1656 for one dayes worke of himselfe at 1*s.* 6*d.* and for 5 dayes worke of 2 men each of them at 1*s.* a peece per diem and for one day worke of one man at 1*s.* per diem	00	12	06
	paid to Hercules Chadwicke the Carpenter the 12th of March 1656 for 4 dayes worke of twoe men at 1*s.* a peece per diem	00	08	00
	paid the 18th of March 1656 for 4 Iron hookes for the hanginge of Bacon	00	00	06
	paid to James Barrett the 18th of March 1656 for a longe drawe Table for the use of the hospitall	04	00	00
	paid to James Barrett the same tyme for 100 of Lattes	00	03	00
	paid more to him the same tyme for a peece of timber to mend the broken beame in the great parloure	00	07	00
	[TOTAL:]	07	07	11
f. 8^{v}	Paid to John Mills the 19° of March 1656 in part for Flaggs for the use of the hospitall	03	00	00
	paid the 21° of March 1656 to Henry Walker the Whiter for 10 dayes worke of one man	00	10	00
	paid to Henry Walker the 23th of March 1656 for a day worke and a peece	00	01	04
	[TOTAL:]	03	11	04
	Wee Whose names are subscribed doe find that m^{r} Richard Dutton hath received of and from m^{r} James Lightbowne since the makeinge of his last account which was the 30th day of January last past before this 30th of March 1657 the just sume of Three score and Tenn pounds, wee say	70	00	00

		£	s.	d.
	And wee doe alsoe find that the said m^{r} Richard Dutton hath disbursed since the makeinge of his aforesaid account as may appeare by this booke in perticulers, and by his booke of weekely paymentes the summe of Fortie foure pounds Fifteene shillings and foure pence, over and besides the summe of Tenn pounds seaventeene shillings and Nyne pence, which together are	55	13	01
	Which said Tenn pounds seaventeene shillings nyne pence was due to m^{r} Dutton at his last account	14	06	11

Soe that there remaineth this 30th of March 1657 in the hands of the said m^{r} Richard Dutton due to the hospitall the Just summe of Fourteene pounds six shillings and Eleaven pence
Examined by us
Henry Wrigley
Raphe Worsley
These accounts were seene and allowed upon the 30th day of March 1657 being Easter Monday by us
Edmund Hopwood
Richard Radcliffe
John Tildsley
John Okey

		£	s.	d.
f. 9	Paid to Edward Platt the Mason the 4th of Aprill 1657 for one dayes worke of 2 men either of them at 1*s.* 2*d.* per diem, and for 5 dayes worke of one man at 1*s.* per diem	00	07	04
	given to the worke men in drinke 9th of Aprill 1657	00	00	02
	paid to Henry Walker the Whiter the 11th of Aprill 1657 for 17 dayes worke of one man beinge in the great parloure in the hospitall	00	17	00
	paid the 11th of Aprill 1657 for a grater for the use of the hospitall	00	00	03
	paid to Henry Walker the Whiter the 18th of Aprill 1657 for 12 dayes worke and ½ of one man in the great parloure in the hospitall	00	12	06
	paid the 18th of Aprill 1657 for halfe a dozen of trenchers for the use of the hospitall	00	00	11
	paid the 24th of Aprill 1657 to Thomas Bourne for dresseinge and Coloureinge redd three dozen of calfe skins for the use of the hospitall at 10*s.* per dozen	01	10	00
	paid to Henry Walker the Whiter the 25th of Aprill 1657 for 16 dayes worke of one man teareinge the kitchin and some other worke at 1*s.* per diem	00	16	00
	paid to John Ryland the 2° of May 1657 for painting stuffe for the great parloure	00	18	00
	paid the 2° of May for one hoope of Leather patches	00	01	08
	paid the 7th of May 1657 to Lawrance Garner for a pye-plate weighinge 2^{li} & 10 ounces for the use of the hospitall	00	03	06
	paid to Henry Walker the Whiter the 13th of May 1657 for 6 dayes worke and ½ of one man pointinge and whiteinge the kitchin	00	06	06
	paid to Jeremy Woosencroft the 14th of May 1657 for makeinge a hooke for the kitchin doore, & a plate for a forme in the Hall	00	00	08
	paid to Samuell Winter the 14th of May 1657 for nailes for the use of the Hospitall	00	06	06

		£	s.	d.
	paid to James Seddon the 23th of May 1657 for staveing a ladder, falling an Ash and some other odd worke	00	03	00
	paid to Richard Martinscroft the 10th of June 1657 for Claspeinge bookes in the Library	00	06	00
	paid 11th of June 1657 to m^{r} Nicholas Hawettes man for leadinge foure loade of Sand	00	01	10
	paid the 12th of June 1657 to James Ouldham for a 11 load of sand for the use of the hospitall	00	07	04
	[TOTAL:]	06	19	02
f. 9^{v}	Paid to Raphe Smith the Breekelayer the 13th of June 1657 for eight dayes worke of a man to make morter	00	08	00
	paid to John Greaves the 20th day of June 1657 for Carriage of one Loade of Flaggs from George Milles	00	06	00
	paid to James Greaves the twentieth of June 1657 for the Carriage of a Loade of Flaggs from George Milles	00	06	00
	paid to John Cheetam the Twentieth of June 1657 for the Carriage of a Loade of flaggs from George Milles	00	06	00
	paid to Richard Martinscroft the 23th of June 1657 for Chaneinge bookes in the Library	00	03	06
	paid to the Smith the 23th of June 1657 for makeinge a Style for the great dyall	00	02	03
	paid to Gilbert Smith the 27th of June 1657 for 38^{li} of Floore nailes for the use of the hospitall	00	12	08
	paid to Richard Martinscroft the 29th of June 1657 for draweinge the great diall belonginge to the Hospitall	00	06	08
	paid the 30th of June 1657 for 8^{li} of Leade to soder the Style in the great dyall	00	01	04
	paid to Charles Lort the 1° of July 1657 for carriage of a Loade of Flaggs from George Mills	00	06	00
	paid to John Cheetam the First of July 1657 for the Carriage of a Loade of Flaggs from George Mills	00	06	00
	paid to George Booth the Third of July 1657 for paintinge stuffe for the great dyall as may appeare by his note	00	08	00
	paid to George Milles the 4th of July 1657 upon account for Flaggs	00	10	00
	[TOTAL:]	04	02	05
f. 10	Paid the 4th of July 1657 to John Cheetham for the Carriage of a Loade of Flaggs from George Mills	00	06	00
	paid to John Lort the 4th of July 1657 for the Carriage of a Loade of Flaggs from George Mills	00	06	00
	paid to Jonathan Greene the 4th of July 1657 for the Carriage of a Loade of Flaggs from George Mills	00	06	00
	paid to Edward Platt the 4th of July 1657 for 60 Loade of Stone for the use of the hospitall at 1*s.* per Loade [the stone at 1*s.* 2*d.* per loade [crossed through]] the leadeinge	06	10	00

		£	s.	d.
	paid to Edward Platt the Mason the same tyme for 9 dayes worke of himselfe at 1*s.* 4*d.* per diem and for 3 dayes worke of his man at 1*s.* per diem	00	15	00
	paid to Raphe Smith the Breekelayer the 4th of July 1657 for 15 dayes worke of a man for the breeke wall in the Court	00	15	00
	paid to him the same tyme, for part of a dayes worke makeinge Morter	00	00	09
	paid to Henry Walker the 4th of July 1657 for 4 dayes worke about the great diall	00	04	00
	paid the 6th of July 1657 for twoe Load of Lyme	00	03	00
	paid the 10th of July 1657 for 6 pound of Leade to soder with	00	01	00
	paid to John Cheetham the 11th of July 1657 for the Carriage of a Loade of Slate from George Milles	00	06	00
	paid to Raphe Smith the Breekelayer the 11th of July 1657 for a weekes worke of himselfe at 1*s.* 2*d.* per diem, and for a weeks worke of 2 men either of them at 1*s.* per diem, & for 5 dayes worke of another man at 1*s.* per diem, and for a weekes worke of an other at 7*d.* per diem	01	07	06
	paid to Edward Platt the Mason the 11th of July 1657 for a weekes worke of himselfe at 1*s.* 4*d.* per diem, & for 5 dayes worke of one man at 1*s.* 2*d.* per diem & for 5 dayes worke of another man at 1*s.* per diem & for 4 dayes worke of another man at 1*s.* per diem	01	02	10
	paid John Piersevall the 11th of July 1657 for bandes & gudgeons for the doores in the new breeke wall	00	13	00
	paid the 13th of July 1657 for 6 Load of Sand	00	04	00
	paid the 14th of July 1657 for 4 loade of Clay	00	02	00
	paid the 15th of July 1657 for foure spradds	00	00	05
	[TOTAL:]	13	02	06
f. 10v	Paid the 15th of July 1657 for 4li of Leade for soder, to soder the gudgeons in the doores of the new breeke walles	00	00	08
	paid the 15th of July 1657 for a pecke of Leather patches	00	00	05
	paid the 18th of July 1657 to Henry Walker the Whiter for teereinge the hall in the hospitall	00	16	00
	given the same tyme to the Workemen in drinke	00	00	03
	paid to Raphe Smith the Breekelayer the 18th of July 1657 for a weekes worke of one man at 1*s.* 2*d.* per diem, and for a weekes worke of 3 men at 1*s.* a peece per diem, and for a weekes worke of a boy at 7*d.* per diem at the new breeke wall	01	08	06
	paid the 18th of July 1657 to John Cheetham for the Carriage of a Loade of Flaggs from George Mills	00	06	00
	paid to the Breekelayer the 21o July 1657 for part of a daye worke of one man, in drawinge the breeke wall	00	00	09
	paid the 22o of July 1657 for a Style for the litle dyall belonginge to the Hospitall	00	00	06

		£	*s.*	*d.*
	paid to Richard Whitworth the 25th of July 1657 for the Carriage of a Loade of Flaggs from George Mills	00	06	00
	paid to John Cheetham the 25th of July 1657 for the Carriage of a Load of Slate from George Mills	00	06	00
	paid the 31° of July 1657 for a Chamber pott	00	02	04
	paid the 3° of August 1657 for a Quire of Capp paper to bee Covers for the Globes	00	00	04
	paid the same tyme for makeinge the Covers for the Gloabes	00	00	06
	paid the 3° of August 1657 for Leadinge 8 Cart loade & ½ of paveing stones bought of m^{r} Holbroocke for the use of the hospitall	00	02	11
	paid to m^{r} Holbroocke the 6° of August 1657 for the aforesaid stones	00	02	10
	paid to Henry Walker the Whiter the 8th of August 1657 for 5 dayes worke of 2 men at 1*s.* a peece per diem and for 2 dayes worke of one man at 1*s.* per diem in teereinge & whiteinge the hall	00	12	00
	paid the 8th of August 1657 for ½ a hoope of haire for the use of the hospitall	00	00	06
	[TOTAL:]	04	06	06
f. 11	Paid to John Cheetham the 8th of August 1657 for the Carriage of a Load of Slate from George Milles	00	06	00
	paid to Edward Platt the Mason the 8th of August 1657 for 12 dayes worke and ½ of himselfe at 1*s.* 4*d.* per diem, and for 5 dayes worke and ½ of one man at 1*s.* 2*d.* per diem and for 11 dayes worke of another man at 1*s.* per diem and for 7 dayes worke of another man at 1*s.* per diem	02	01	00
	paid the 15th of August 1657 to John Cheetham for a Loade of Slate for the use of the hospitall	00	08	02
	paid to Thomas Matley the 15th of August 1657 for five dayes worke and part of another in guildinge 2 dyalles for the hospitall	00	05	06
	paid for paintinge stuffe & oyle for the dyalles	00	02	11
	paid the 15th of August 1657 for 2 bookes and ½ for the guildinge of the dyalles	00	06	03
	paid to Edward Platt the Mason the 15th August 1657 for 6 dayes worke of himselfe at 1*s.* 4*d.* per diem, and for 6 dayes worke of one man at 1*s.* 2*d.* per diem, and for 6 dayes worke of 2 men either of them at 1*s.* a peece per diem and for 4 dayes worke of one man at 1*s.* per diem	01	11	00
	paid to John Piersevall the Smith the 19th of August 1657 for 18 score and ½ weight of Iron worke for the new Poarch and the new staires at 4*d.* ½ per^{li} as may appeare by his note	06	15	06
	paid to John Piersevall the Smith the 28th of August 1657 for 24^{li} & ½ weight of Iron worke for the new poarch	00	10	02
	paid to Edward Platt the 29th of August 1657 for a weekes worke of himselfe at 1*s.* 4*d.* per diem and for a weekes worke of 3 men at 1*s.* a peece per diem, and for 2 dayes worke of one man at 1*s.* per diem	01	08	00

		£	*s.*	*d.*
	paid to James Barrett the 31° of August 1657 for Lattes and a peece of wood to stave the Ladder	00	08	04
	paid to James Barrett the same tyme for 200 of pannelles	02	10	00
	paid the 1° of September 1657 for a Mapp to wash the Library floore	00	00	08
	paid & given to the workemen in drinke the 2° Sept 57	00	00	04
	paid to John Piersevall the 4th of September 1657 for 39^{li} & ½ weight of great nailes for the new poarch doore at 6*d.* per^{li}	00	19	09
	paid for 4 spradds 4th September 1657 for nayleinge a sparr in the hall	00	00	06
	[TOTAL:]	17	14	01
f. 11^{v}	Paid to John Chetham the 5th of September 1657 for the Carriage of a Loade of Slate from George Milles	00	06	00
	paid the 5th of September 1657 for 500 of mungrill nayles for the use of the hospitall	00	02	10
	paid to Edward Platt the Mason the 5th of September 1657 for 3 dayes worke & ½ of himselfe at 1*s.* 4*d.* per diem and for 6 dayes worke of one man at 1*s.* per diem and for 4 dayes worke of another man at 1*s.* per diem	00	14	08
	paid to John Piersevall the Smith the 12th of September 1657 for 13^{li} weight of nayles for the new poarch doore at 6*d.* per ^{li}	00	06	06
	paid to him the same tyme for a Hammer for the Hall doore	00	01	00
	paid to him the same tyme for 8^{li} weight of window rodds at 4*d.* ½ per^{li}	00	03	00
	paid to Hercules Chadwicke the Carpenter the 12th of September 1657 for 8 dayes worke makeinge the doores in the new poarch, & layinge the Joystes at 1*s.* 6*d.* per diem	00	12	00
	paid to Edward Platt the Mason the 12th September 1657 for 5 dayes worke and ½ of himselfe at 1*s.* 4*d.* per diem, and for 5 dayes worke & ½ of one man at 1*s.* 2*d.* per diem, and for 5 dayes worke of 3 men at 1*s.* a peece per diem, and for 2 dayes worke of one man at 1*s.* per diem	01	10	02
	paid to John Piersevall the 17th of September 1657 for Smith worke for the new poarch, as may appeare by his note	00	11	00
	paid to John Chetham the 19th of September 1657 for a Loade of Slate	00	08	00
	paid to Hercules Chadwicke the Carpenter the 19th of September 1657 for a weekes worke of himselfe at 1*s.* 6*d.* per diem, and for a weekes worke of one man at 1*s.* per diem	00	15	00
	paid to Edward Platt the Mason the 19th of September 1657 for a weekes worke of himselfe at 1*s.* 4*d.* per diem and for a day worke of a man at 1*s.* 2*d.* per diem, & for 5 dayes worke of 2 men each of them at 1*s.* per diem	00	19	02
	paid to William Williamson the 26th September 1657 for 45 foote of glasse and 60 quarrelles for the new porch at 4*d.* ½ per foote	00	18	04
	[TOTAL:]	07	07	08

		£	*s.*	*d.*
f. 12	Paid to Hercules Chadwicke the Carpenter the 26th of September 1657 for a weekes worke of himselfe at 1*s.* 6*d.* per diem, and for a weekes worke of a man at 1*s.* per diem	00	15	00
	paid to John Chetham the 26th of September 1657 for twoe Loade of Slate	00	16	00
	paid to Edward Platt the Mason the 26 of September 1657 for 5 dayes worke of himselfe at 1*s.* 4*d.* per diem, and for 5 dayes of one man at 1*s.* per diem and for 2 dayes of a man at 1*s.* per diem, and for one day worke of a man at 1*s.* 2*d.* per diem	00	14	10
	paid to Thomas Sydebotham the Plumer the 29th of September 1657 for 18 pound of Lead to soder with	00	03	00
	paid the 1° October 1657 for 2 loade of Clay	00	01	00
	paid to John Swindell the 3° October 1657 for one Loade of lyme	00	01	08
	paid Hercules Chadwicke the Carpenter the 3° September 1657 for 5 dayes worke and ½ of himselfe at 1*s.* 6*d.* per diem, and for 5 dayes worke and ½ of a man at 1*s.* per diem and for 2 dayes of another man at 1*s.* per diem and for one day worke of another man at 1*s.* per diem	00	17	03
	paid Edward Platt the 3° October 1657 for 5 dayes worke of himselfe at 1*s.* 4*d.* per diem and for 6 dayes worke of a man at 1*s.* per diem and for 5 dayes worke of another man at 1*s.* per diem	00	17	08
	paid Edward Platt the same tyme for 4 loade of stone at 2*s.* 2*d.* per loade	00	08	08
	paid Henry Walker the 3° October 1657 for 3 dayes worke of 2 men at 1*s.* a peece per diem	00	06	00
	paid the 3° October 1657 for haire to make morter	00	03	00
	paid the 5th of October 1657 for 5 loade of lyme at 1*s.* 8*d.* per loade	00	08	04
	paid for 500th of Mungrelles and for 500th of Stone nayles the 5th of October 1657	00	04	06
	paid the same tyme for a Mapp to wash the Library floore	00	00	07
	paid the 7th of October 1657 to Edward Cleaton for 5 Loade of lyme at 1*s.* 8*d.* per loade	00	08	04
	Given to the workemen in drinke the 9th October 1657	00	00	06
	paid to Hercules Chadwicke the Carpenter the 10th of October 1657 for a weekes worke of himselfe at 1*s.* 6*d.* per diem, and for a weekes worke of 2 men either of them at 1*s.* per diem	01	01	00
	[TOTAL:]	07	07	04
f. 12^{v}	Paid the 10th of October 1657 to Edward Cleaton for 4 Loade of lyme at 1*s.* 8*d.* per loade	00	06	06
	paid to Edward Williamson the 10th of October 1657 some worke done at a diall for the use of the hospitall	00	00	06
	paid Edward Platt the Mason the 10th October 1657 for 5 dayes worke of himselfe at 1*s.* 4*d.* per diem and for 4 dayes worke & ½ of one man at 1*s.* 2*d.* per diem, and for 6 dayes worke of another man at 1*s.* per diem, & for 4 dayes worke of another at 1*s.* per diem, and for 3 dayes & ½ of another at 1*s.* per diem	01	10	05

		£	s.	d.
	paid to John Piersevall the Smith the 10th October 1657 for alteringe windowe rodds	00	03	00
	paid to John Swindell the 12th of October 1657 for 3 loade of Lyme at 1*s.* 8*d.* per loade	00	05	00
	paid the 12th October 1657 for ½ a hoope of patches for the use of the hospitall	00	00	10
	paid the 13th of October 1657 for 6 Loade of Lyme at 1*s.* 8*d.* per loade	00	10	00
	paid the 13th of October 1657 to John Cheetham for a Loade of Slate	00	08	00
	paid the 14 of October 1657 to John Swindelles for 2 loade of Lyme	00	03	04
	paid the 16 of October 1657 the chiefe rent due to Col[one]l Birch & mr Whitworth from the hospitall the 29th September last	00	03	09
	paid to George Milles the 17th of October 1657 for 4 loade of Slate as they were bought at the delfe	00	08	06
	paid to Henry Walker the Whiter the 17th of October 1657 for 4 dayes worke and ½ of 2 men either of them at 1*s.* per diem	00	09	00
	paid the same tyme for ½ a hoope of haire	00	00	06
	paid the 17th October 1657 to Edward Cleaton for 4 Loade of Lyme at 1*s.* 8*d.* per loade	00	06	08
	paid to John Piersevall the Smith the 17th October 1657 for alteringe some Window rodds	00	02	08
	paid the 17th October 1657 to Francis Cottrell for one Loade of lyme	00	01	08
	paid to Hercules Chadwicke the Carpenter 17th of October 1657 for a weekes worke of himselfe at 1*s.* 6*d.* per diem, & for 7 dayes worke of one man at 1*s.* per diem	00	16	00
	[TOTAL:]	05	16	04
f. 13	Paid to Edward Platt the Mason the 17th of October 1657 for a weekes worke of himselfe at 1*s.* 4*d.* per diem & for 2 dayes worke of one man at 1*s.* 2*d.* per diem & for 4 dayes worke of another man at 1*s.* per diem & for 3 dayes worke & ½ of another man at 1*s.* per diem	00	17	10
	paid & given to the workemen in drinke 17th October 1657	00	00	06
	paid the 17th October 1657 to Henry Walker for layinge 2 Casementes in redd	00	00	08
	paid to Edward Cleaton the 21° October 1657 for 4 loade of Lyme at 1*s.* 8*d.* per loade	00	06	08
	paid to John Piersevall the Smith the 23th October 1657 for a fire shovell and tongs for the Hall	00	05	04
	paid to him the same tyme for a double Casement, and for mendinge another Casement	00	04	06
	paid to John Walker the Whiter the 23° October 1657 for 2 dayes worke at 1*s.* per diem	00	02	00

		£	*s.*	*d.*
	paid the 23th of October 1657 for a Locke & a Key for the new poarch doore	00	02	10
	paid to John Swindell the 24th of October 1657 for twoe loade of Lyme	00	03	03
	paid to Hercules Chadwicke the Carpenter the 24th of October 1657 for a weekes worke of himselfe at 1*s.* 6*d.* per diem and for a weekes worke of a man at 1*s.* per diem	00	15	00
	paid to Edward Platt the Mason the 24th of October 1657 for 2 dayes worke of himselfe at 1*s.* 4*d.* per diem and for 5 dayes worke of one man at 1*s.* 2*d.* per diem and for 6 dayes worke of one man at 1*s.* per diem & for 2 dayes worke of another man at 1*s.* per diem	00	16	06
	paid the 26 October 1657 for twoe Cromps for the gatehouse Chimney	00	01	02
	paid the same tyme for a litle fire shovell	00	00	10
	paid the 26 of October 1657 for carriage of the Leade for the new staire case from Salford	00	00	06
	paid to Thomas Sydebotham the 28th of October 1657 for 411^{li} weight of leade for the new staire case at 2*d.* per pound	04	01	10
	paid more to him the same tyme for Eleven score and 17^{li} weight of Leade for gutters in the gate house at 2*d.* per^{li}	01	16	02
	paid to Edward Cleaton the 29° October 1657 for 4 Loade of lyme at 1*s.* 8*d.* per loade	00	06	08
	[TOTAL:]	10	02	03
f. 13^{v}	Paid to Hercules Chadwicke the Carpenter the 29th of October 1657 for 3 dayes worke of himselfe at 1*s.* 6*d.* per diem, & for 3 dayes worke & ½ of a man at 1*s.* per diem	00	08	00
	paid to Henry Walker the Whiter the 30th of October 1657 for 3 dayes worke & ½ of himselfe at 1*s.* per diem	00	03	06
	paid to Edward Platt the Mason the 30th of October 1657 for 3 dayes worke of one man at 1*s.* per diem, & for 2 dayes worke of another man at 1*s.* per diem	00	05	00
	paid to Raphe Smith the Breeke Layer the 30th October 1657 for makeinge an Oven and setinge the topp on the garden doore [One line of text has been rubbed away]	00	08	08
	paid the 4th of November 1657 for Leadinge 5 loade of Slate bought of Richard Karsley	00	02	06
	paid the 4th of November 1657 for 5 burne of Mosse	00	01	05
	paid to Henry Walker the Whiter the 5th of November 1657 for one day of worke & a peece	00	01	04
	paid to John Lort the 7th of November 1657 for 3 loade of Slate at 9*s.* per loade	01	07	00
	paid more to John Lort the same tyme for 4 loade of Slate at 8*s.* 3*d.* per loade	01	13	00
	paid the same tyme to Redford for a Wheelebarrowe	00	03	00
	paid to Gilbert Smith the 7th of November 1657 for nayles as may appeare by his note	00	16	11

		£	s.	d.
	paid the 7th of November 1657 for Leather patches	00	00	04
	paid to Charles Lort the 11th of November 1657 for a Loade of Slate	00	09	00
	paid the 12th of November 1657 for 4 burne of Mosse	00	01	00
	paid to Richard Martinscroft the 13th of November 1657 for Cheaneinge bookes in the Library	00	04	08
	paid to him the same tyme for draweinge the litle wall diall	00	03	00
	paid the 13th of November 1657 for more Mosse	00	00	09
	paid Richard Karsley the 14th of November 1657 for 5 loade of Slate for the gatehouse at 8*s.* 2*d.* per load and 2*d.* overe	02	01	00
	paid to him the same tyme for Slateinge the gate house beinge 102 square yards & for 10 yards which was taken downe to make roome for the new staire case, & for 4 yards at Alice Deane house at 4*d.* per yard	01	18	08
	[TOTAL:]	10	08	09
f. 14	Paid to Richard Karsley the 14th November 1657 for 2 dayes worke of 2 men in Moseinge and mendinge	00	04	00
	paid to Daniell Digle the 14th of November 1657 for 2 dayes worke removeinge some Rubbidge and makeinge way to the Church	00	02	00
	paid to Henry Walker the 16th day of November 1657 for Coloureinge a Casement for the new porch	00	00	04
	paid the 16th of November 1657 for Cleanseinge the Schole Court	00	00	04
	paid to Daniell Digle the 16th of November 1657 for removeinge more rubbidge	00	01	00
	paid to Edward Platt the Mason the 17th of November 1657 for 3 Dayes worke of a man laying flaggs and some other worke	00	03	06
	paid the 20th of November 1657 to Raphe Wollen for 6 pound weight of wyre to chaine bookes in the Library	00	10	00
	paid to Thurstan Digle the 20th of November 1657 for 2000 of stone nailes for the use of the hospitall	00	03	04
	paid to Jeremy Woosencroft the 25th of November 1657 for makeinge a new key & mendinge a Locke for mr Browns Chamber doore	00	00	10
	paid to Willaim Strettell the 25th November for 22 hoopes of haire for the use of the hospitall	01	00	00
	paid the 26° November 1657 for shoeing a wheelebarrow	00	03	04
	paid to James Seddon the 26 November 1657 for setinge stoopes & railes in the garden	00	06	00
	paid to James Bradshawe the 7th December 1657 for Leadinge 12 loade of sand for flagging the kitchin	00	03	04
	paid to James Seddon the 7th of November 1657 for makeinge pendices over the houses of office	00	02	00
	paid to James Barrett the 9th December 1657 for Lattes and pinwood for repaireinge the gatehouse as may appeare by his note	01	09	10
	paid to Henry Walker the Whiter the 12th December 1657 for one day worke of 2 men in pointinge windows in the new staire case	00	02	00

		£	s.	d.
	paid James Seddon the 13 of December 1657 for a puding reele and some other worke	00	01	00
	paid Edward Platt the Mason the 25th December 1657 for flagging 81 yards square at 4*d.* per yard	01	07	00
	paid to him the same tyme for one day worke of a man prepareinge the floore for flagginge	00	01	00
	[TOTAL:]	06	00	10
f. 14v	Given the Brewer the 1° of January 1657 for a New Yeares gift	00	01	00
	paid to George Mills the 8th of January 1657 in full for tenn Loades of Flaggs	00	06	00
	paid to James Barrett the 11th of January 1657 for 66 yardes of Boards at 7*d.* per yard	01	18	06
	paid to him the same tyme for 32 yards of Rayles at 3*d.* ½ per yard	00	09	00
	paid William Williamson the Glasier the 11th of January 1657 for 63 foote and 36 quarrells of new glasse for the new staire case at 4*d.* ½ per foote	01	05	10
	paid to him the same tyme for some other odd worke	00	04	00
	paid to James Seddon the Carpenter the 21° of January 1657 for 3 dayes worke layinge sleepers in the upper end of the Hall to board on	00	03	00
	paid to Edward Platt the Mason the 23th January 1657 for one dayes worke & ½ of one man at 1*s.* 2*d.* per diem, and for one day and a peece of 3 men each of them at 1*s.* per diem	00	05	00
	paid to mr Samuell Harmar the 26th of January 1657 for a flagg to lay in the great Chamber Chymney	00	09	00
	paid the 30th January 1657 for 2li of floore nayles	00	00	08
	paid to James Barrett the 13th of February 1657 for 43 yards of Rachmentes at 3*d.* ½ per yard	00	12	06
	paid to James Bradshawe the 14th of February 1657 for removeinge 699 loade of Rubbadge out of the Court in the Hospitall at 1*d.* ½ per load	04	04	10
	paid to James Bradshawe the 17th February 1657 for removeinge 47 Cart load of rubbage out of the Court and the Alley at the breeke wall side at 1*s.* ½ per loade	00	04	11
	paid to Edward Platt the Mason 17th February 1657 for a day worke and a peece and twoe men and himselfe	00	04	00
	paid to James Seddon the Carpenter the 18th February 1657 for 3 dayes worke setinge Railes in the garden	00	03	00
	[TOTAL:]	10	11	03
f. 15	Paid to James Bradshawe the 27th February 1657 for removeinge 30 loade of Rubbage at 1*d.* ½ per loade	00	03	07
	paid to him the same tyme for a day worke of himselfe in removeinge Rubbadge	00	01	06
	paid to John Piersevall the Smith the 3° March 1657 for twoe double Casementes in the gallary at 1*s.* 1*d.* per foote, and for makeinge windowe rodds as may appeare by his note	01	11	03

		£	*s.*	*d.*
	paid to William Williamson the 3° of March 1657 for 61 foote of glasse in the gallary at 4*d.* ½ per foote and for 77 quarrelles at 1*s.* 1*d.* per score	01	07	00
	paid the 3° of March 1657 for one pound of glue	00	00	04
	paid to James Seddon the Carpenter the 4th March 1657 for 4 dayes worke and a peece makeinge windowe stooles in the great Chamber, and cuting the Arch beames feete	00	04	04
	paid to Thurstan Digle the 9th of March 1657 for 4 paire of bands, latches & catches for the seeled doores in the great Chamber	00	09	00
	paid for nailes to set on the bands	00	00	06
	paid to Jeremy Woosencroft the Smith the 12th of March 1657 for repaireinge 14 Casementes in the great Chamber as may appeare by his note	00	16	00
	paid the 15th of March 1657 for a hoope of haire	00	01	00
	paid to William Williamson the Glasier the 17th of March 1657 for 8 foote of new glasse in the great Chamber at 4*d.* ½ per foote	00	03	06
	paid to him the same tyme for leadeinge 56 foote of glasse at 3*d.* per foote	00	14	00
	paid to him the same tyme for 293 quarrells at 1*s.* 1*d.* per score	00	15	10
	paid more to him the same tyme for pinneinge and leadinge 15 Casementes at 4*d.* per Casement	00	05	00
	paid more to him the same tyme for byndinge and 3 Archpane glasse	00	02	02
	[TOTAL:]	06	15	00
f. 15^{v}	Paid to Jeremy Woosencroft the Smith the 18th of March 1657 for a fire Iron for the great Chamber, weighinge 67^{li} at 3*d.* ½ per pound	00	19	06
	paid to him the same tyme for a double Casement of 5 foote & ¾ at 1*s.* per foote	00	05	08
	paid to the Glasier the 19th of March 1657 for some odd worke	00	01	06
	paid to Jeremy Woosencroft the Smith the 19th of March 1657 for a Casement of 3 foote & ¾ at 1*s.* per foote	00	03	09
	paid the 19th of March 1657 for Leather patches to make syse withall	00	00	06
	paid to Henry Walker the Whiter the 19th of March 1657 for 14 dayes worke of a man in pointing and whiteinge, and layinge coloures in the great Chamber	00	14	00
	paid Edward Platt the Mason the 19th of March 1657 for 3 dayes worke of a man at 1*s.* 2*d.* per diem	00	03	06
	paid to him the same tyme for a day worke of a man at 1*s.* per diem	00	01	00
	paid to Peter Dickson the 19th of March 1657 for seeleing 101 square yards in the great Chamber at 1*s.* per yard and for glueinge 16 pannells at ½^{d} per pannell, & for floreinge 97 square yards in the great Chamber & the Hall at 4*d.* per yard, & for makeing moulds for the Mason worke	06	17	06
	paid to Raphe Smith the 22th of March 1657 for seting the fire Iron in the great Chamber	00	01	00

	£	s.	d.
paid to William Williamson the Glasier the 26° March 1658 for 70 new quarrelles of glasse at 1*s.* 1*d.* per score & for leading 3 foote of old glasse at 3*d.* per foote, & for soderinge and pininge 9 Casementes at 4*d.* per Casement	00	07	06
paid to Henry Walker the Whiter the 27th March 1658 for ½ a day worke of 3 men at 1*s.* a peece per diem & for parte of a day worke of 2 men	00	02	02
paid to Raphe Wollen the 31th of March 1658 for paintinge Coloures for the great chamber & a Chymney as may appeare by his note	00	07	10
[TOTAL:]	10	05	05

		£	s.	d.
f. 16	Paid to Samuell Hollinworth the 31th of March 1658 for ½ a hoope of leather patches to make syse	00	00	06
	paid to Raphe Smith the Breekelayer the 1° of Aprill 1658 for repaireinge the Chimney over the porch	00	05	06
	paid to Henry Walker the Whiter the 2° of Aprill 1658 for 10 dayes worke of a man	00	10	00
	paid to Edward Platt the Mason the 5th of Aprill 1658 for setinge up the litle dyall	00	00	08
	paid the 5th of Aprill 1658 for ½ a hoope of haire to make morter	00	00	06
	paid to Raphe Shelmerdyne the 8th of Aprill 1658 for Coveringe the great Byble in the Hall	00	02	06
	paid to Henry Walker the Whiter the 9th of Aprill 1658 for 4 dayes worke of himselfe	00	04	00
	paid to William Williamson the Glasier the 9th Aprill 1658 for 3 foote of new glasse at 4*d.* ½ the foote, and for other worke	00	04	00
	paid to James Bradshaw the 9th of Aprill 1658 for levellinge the Alley at the breeke wall	00	03	00
	paid to James Barrett the 10th of Aprill 1658 for 30 yards of Ratchmentes at 3*d.* ½ per yard for the use of the hospitall	00	08	09
	paid more to him the same tyme for halfe a hundreth of lattes	00	01	02
	paid more to him the same tyme for a deske standinge in the Hall	00	14	00
	[TOTAL:]	02	14	07

Notes

1 F. Engels, *The Condition of the Working Class in England*, from the first English translation of 1892 quoted in L. D. Bradshaw, ed., *Visitors to Manchester*, 1987, p. 40.

2 L. Toulmin-Smith, *The Itinerary of John Leland in or about the years 1535 to 1543*, 1909, pp. 5–6.

3 Quoted in F. Raines & C. Sutton, *The Life of Humphrey Chetham*, Chetham Society, vol. 2, 1903, p. 259.

4 Quoted in M. Sykes, 'Pages of History', *Country Life*, 20 January 1983, p. 144.

5 C. Morris, ed., *Illustrated Journeys of Celia Fiennes*, 1982, p. 184.

6 L. Toulmin Smith, *loc. cit.*

7 M. Morris, *Medieval Manchester*, 1983, p. 36.

8 Greater Manchester Archaeological Unit, *Annual Report*, 1982–3, pp. 5–8.

9 J. Harvey, *Gothic England*, 1947, p. 34.

10 E. Duffy, *The Voices of Morebath*, 2003, pp. 60–1.

11 This translation in Samuel Hibbert Ware, *History of the Foundations in Manchester of Christ's College, Chetham's Hospital and the Free Grammar School*, vol. 3, 2nd edn. 1848, p. 137.

12 Manchester Central Library L1/51/8/13.

13 W. Farrer et al., *Victoria County History of Lancashire*, vol. 4, 1911, p. 193.

14 P. Hosker, 'The Stanleys of Lathom and ecclesiastical patronage in the north-west of England during the fifteenth century', *Northern History*, vol. 18, 1982, pp. 212–27.

15 M. Girouard, *Life in the English Country House*, 1978, p. 71.

16 F. R. Raines, *History of the Chantries*, Chetham Society, 1862, p. 9.

17 M. Girouard, *op.cit.*, p. 82.

18 M. Morris, *op.cit.*, p. 41.

19 I. Tyers, *Tree Ring Analysis of Timbers from Chetham's Library and School, Long Millgate, Manchester*, English Heritage, 2002.

20 M. Morris, *op. cit.*, p. 39.

21 Minute Book, 22 April 1663.

22 For a table of comparisons of hall sizes in Lancashire and Cheshire see H. Taylor, *Old Halls in Lancashire and Cheshire*, 1884, pp. 17–18.

23 H. A. Hudson, *The Mediaeval Woodwork of Manchester Cathedral*, 1924, pp. 135–40.

24 J. E. Gregan, 'Notes on Humfrey Chetham and his Foundation', *Journal of the British Archaeological Association*, vol. 6, 1851, pp. 294–302.

25 Drawn and engraved by F. Mackenzie from a sketch by C. Pye, Agnew & Zanetti, 1828.

26 GMCRO, K1.

27 'Chantry Priests' Houses and other Medieval Lodgings', *Medieval Archaeology*, no. 3, 1959, pp. 216–58.

28 H. Taylor, *op.cit.*, p. 44.

29 'Lord I have loved the habitation of thy house', Psalm 26, verse 8.

30 *see* E. F. Letts, 'Warden Huntyngton', *TLCAS*, vol. 2, 1884, pp. 92–104, for a discussion of his life, origins and memorial brass.

31 quoted in E. F. Letts, *op. cit*, pp. 103–4.

32 F. R. Raines, *The Rectors of Manchester and the Wardens of the Collegiate Church of that Town*, Chetham Society, 1885, pp. 30–1.

33 *see* M. K. Jones and M. G. Underwood, *The King's Mother, Lady Margaret Beaufort Countess of Richmond and Derby*, 1992.

34 for a discussion of Bromflet's work *see* C. Grössinger, 'The relationship between Manchester Cathedral misericords and those in Ripon Cathedral and Beverly Minster', *TLCAS*, 2002, pp. 27–47.

35 quoted in F. R. Raines, *op. cit.*, p. 42.

36 Farrer et al., *op. cit.*, p. 502.

37 R. Hollingworth, *Mancuniensis*, 1650s, published 1839, p. 50.

38 Unpublished research by Joanna Booth.

39 Chetham's Library, Manchester.

40 R. Hollingworth, *op. cit*, p. 63.

41 PRO SP 12/278/18, reproduced in B. Coward, *The Stanleys: Lords Stanley and Earls of Derby*, 1983, p. 263.

42 J. E. Bailey, ed., *Diary for the Years 1595–1601 of Dr John Dee*, privately printed book, 1880, p. 47.

43 J. E. Bailey, ed., *op cit.*, p. 58.

44 Quoted in *Palatine Notebook*, vol. 1, 1881, p. 47.

45 Farrer et al, *op. cit.*, p. 178n.

46 W. Beaumont, ed., *A Discourse of the Warr in Lancashire*, Chetham Society, 1864, p. 11.

47 for an account of Stanley fortunes in the Civil War and after see B. Coward, *op. cit.*

48 *see* F. R. Raines and C. W. Sutton, 'The Life of Humphrey Chetham', *Chetham Society*, 2 vols, 1903, and S. Guscott, 'Humphrey Chetham 1580–1653: Fortune, Politics and Mercantile Culture in Seventeenth-Century Britain', *Chetham Society*, 2003.

49 B. G. Blackwood, 'The Lancashire Gentry and the Great Rebellion', *Chetham Society*, vol. 35, 1978, p. 18.

50 T. Wyke, '"So Honest a Physiognomy": Memorialising Humphrey Chetham', *TLCAS*, forthcoming.

51 Chetham's Library, Allen Deeds Parcel N (302) (ii).

52 *ibid.*

53 Raines & Sutton, *op. cit.*, vol. 1, p. 195.

54 J. Stanning, ed., *The Lancashire Royalist Composition Papers*, Record Society of Lancashire and Cheshire, 1892, p. 174

55 Chetham's Library C/COLLEGE/2.

56 B. S. Capp, *The Fifth Monarchy Men*, 1972, pp. 78–9.

57 R. Parkinson, ed., *The Life of Adam Martindale written by Himself*, Chetham Society, 1845, p. 75.

58 quoted in P. F. Gura, *A Glimpse of Sion's Glory*, 1984, p. 94

59 T. Dowley, 'John Wigan and the first Baptists of Manchester', *Baptist Quarterly*, N.S. vol. 25, 1973–4, p. 153.

60 *The history of the worthies of England*, 1662, sig. R1.

61 B. H. Streeter, *The Chained Library*, 1931, pp. 298–9.

62 quoted in Raines & Sutton, *op. cit.*, p. 252.

63 Minute Book, 27 March 1654.

64 Chetham's Library C/COLLEGE/6.

65 Chetham's Library C/COLLEGE/10.

66 Chetham's Library Allen Deeds parcel S (1).

67 S. Guscott, *op. cit*, p. 271.

68 Minute Book, 5 November 1655.

69 Minute Book, *loc. cit.*

70 Chetham's Library, Allen Deeds, parcel N (299).

71 Chetham's Library, Allen Deeds parcel S (2).

72 *see* J. P. Earwaker, ed., *The Constables Accounts of the Manor of Manchester from the year 1612 to the year 1647, and from the year 1743 to the year 1776*, 1892.

73 Minute Book, 22 April 1663.

74 I am indebted to Michael Powell, who put his research on Martinscrofte and the library furnishings at my disposal.

75 Henry Newcome, *The Diary of the Rev. Henry Newcome from September 30, 1661 to September 29, 1663*, Chetham's Society, 1849, p. 29.

76 Minute Book, 27 March 1665.

77 Minute Book, 16 May 1666.

78 W. Mullis, *A Brief Account of the Blue Coat Hospital and Public Library in The College, Manchester founded by Humphrey Chetham Esq. in the year 1651*, 1826.

79 *loc. cit.*

80 I am grateful to Claire Gapper for her advice on the plasterwork.

81 Minute Book, 4 October 1675; 27 March 1676.

82 by Hannah Hartwell of St Paul's Cathedral, London, to whom I am indebted for information about parallels with Gibbons' workshop.

83 *see* Stefanie Knoell, 'An Eternal Academic Community: Oxford Memorials 1580–1680', *Church Monuments*, vol. 26, 2001, pp. 58–64.

84 Chetham's library, C/LIB/AC/2 (ii).

85 Minute Book, 9 August 1671.

86 A. Oswald, 'Chetham's Hospital Furniture', *Country Life*, 1 September 1934, p. 230.

87 Minute Book, 5 May 1667.

88 T. Stanley Ball, 'Chetham Hospital Silver Plate', *TLCAS*, vol. 26, 1908, pp. 27–34

89 David Porter, pers. comm.

90 Minute Book, 15 May 1661.

91 Minute Book, 6 October 1658.

92 W. Croston, *Nooks and Corners of Lancashire and Cheshire*, 1882, p. 159.

93 *Palatine Notebook*, vol. 1, 1881, p. 108.

94 Minute Book, 22 April 1663.

95 Minute Book, 27 March 1665.

96 Chetham's Library, Allen Deeds parcel S (1).

97 J. P. Earwaker, ed., *Manchester Court Leet Records*, vol. 4, 1887, p. 188.

98 Minute Book, 6 April 1656.

99 J. P. Earwaker, ed., *Manchester Court Leet Records*, vol. 2, 1884, pp. 333, 335.

100 *Palatine Notebook*, vol. 1, 1881, p. 210.

101 W. E. Axon, *Manchester A Hundred Years Ago: Being a Reprint of A Description of Manchester by a Native of the Town James Ogden, Published in 1783*, 1887, p. 21.

102 W. Harrison, 'The Old House of Correction at Hunt's Bank, Manchester', *TLCAS*, vol. 3, 1885, pp. 89–110.

103 J. E. Bailey, ed., *op.cit.*, p. 64.

104 Chetham's Library, C/COLLEGE/3.

105 Chetham's Library, C/COLLEGE/8.

106 Chetham's Library C/COLLEGE/3.

107 J. P. Earwaker, ed., *The Constables Accounts of the Manor of Manchester*, vol. 2, 1892, pp. 195, 215.

108 Minute Book, 27 May 1662.

109 H. Taylor, *op. cit.*, pp. 31–46.

110 A. Emery, *Greater Medieval Houses of England and Wales 1300–1500* (1996), pp. 219–24.

111 W. A. Pantin, 'Chantry Priests Houses and other Medieval Lodgings', *Medieval Archaeology*, no. 3 (1959), pp. 216–258.

112 W. A. Pantin, *op. cit.*, p. 258.

113 *loc. cit.*

114 Comparative plans of lodgings are illustrated in M. Wood, *The English Medieval House* (1965), fig. 58.

115 C. Hussey, 'Wenlock Abbey Shropshire – 1', *Country Life*, 1 December 1960, p. 1283.

116 for other examples and a discussion of north and western crown post roofs see W. J. Smith, *The East Wing, Ordsall Hall, Salford*, GMAU, 1995, pp. 14–16.

117 Chetham's Library, Allen Deeds parcel N(302) (ii).

118 Ian Tyers, *op. cit.*

119 GMCRO, K1.

120 Minute Book, 27 March 1815.

121 *The Builder*, 1847, p. 599.

122 J.E. Gregan, *op. cit.*

123 Minute Book, 29 December 1874.

124 Minute Book, 4 July 1876.

125 Minute Book, 17 April 1876.

126 Minute Book, 1 October 1883.

127 Minute Book, 28 July 1890.

128 H. Taylor, *op. cit.*, p. 42.

Bibliography

ABBREVIATIONS

GMAU Greater Manchester Archaeological Unit

GMCRO Greater Manchester County Record Office

TLCAS Transactions of the Lancashire and Cheshire Antiquarian Society

BIBLIOGRAPHY

W. E. Axon, *Manchester A Hundred Years Ago: Being a Reprint of A Description of Manchester by a Native of the Town James Ogden, Published in 1783*, Manchester, 1887

W. E. Beaumont, ed., *A Discourse of the Warr in Lancashire*, Chetham Society, 1864

B. G. Blackwood, *The Lancashire Gentry and the Great Rebellion*, Chetham Society, 1978

L. D. Bradshawe, *Visitors to Manchester: A Selection of British and Foreign Visitors' Descriptions of Manchester from c. 1538–1865*, Neil Richardson, Swinton, 1987

British Architect and Northern Engineer; 21 July 1876, p. 45; 7 March 1879, p. 104; 18 October 1878, p. 152; 25 October 1878, p. 160

The Builder, 1847 p. 599

B. S. Capp, *The Fifth Monarchy Men, A Study in Seventeenth-Century English Millenarianism,* London, 1972

C. F. Carter, ed., *Manchester and its Region*, Manchester, 1962

Civil Engineer and Architect's Journal, 1845, p. 129

B. Coward, *The Stanleys Lords Stanley and Earls of Derby 1385–1672*, Manchester, 1983

W. Croston, *Nooks and Corners of Lancashire and Cheshire*, Manchester, 1882

T. Dowley, 'John Wigan and the First Baptists of Manchester', *Baptist Quarterly* N.S., vol. 25, 1973–4

E. Duffy, *The Voices of Morebath*, New Haven and London, 2003

J. P. Earwaker, 'The Will of Warden Huntingdon, 1458', *TLCAS*, vol. 3, 1885

J. P. Earwaker, ed., *The Constables' Accounts of the Manor of Manchester from the year 1612 to the year 1647, and from the year 1743 to the year 1776*, 3 vols, Manchester, 1892

J. P. Earwaker, ed., *The Court Leet Records of the Manor of Manchester, from the year 1552 to the year 1686 and from the year 1731 to the year 1846*, 12 vols, Manchester, 1884–90

A. Emery, *Greater Medieval Houses of England and Wales 1300–1500*, Cambridge, 1996

W. Farrer, et al., *The Victoria County History of the County of Lancashire*, vol. 4, London, 1911

M. Girouard, *Life in the English Country House*, New Haven and London, 1978

GMAU, *Annual Report*, Manchester, 1982–3

J. E. Gregan, 'Notes on Humfrey Chetham and his Foundation', *Journal of the British Archaeological Association*, vol. 6, 1851

C. Grossinger, 'The relationship between Manchester Cathedral misericords and those in Ripon Cathedral and Beverly Minster', *TLCAS*, vol. 98, 2002

P. F. Gura, *A Glimpse of Sion's Glory*, Connecticut, 1984

S. Guscott, *Humphrey Chetham 1580–1653: Fortune, Politics and Mercantile Culture in Seventeenth-Century Britain,* Chetham Society, 2003

A. Hamilton Thompson, *The English clergy and their organization in the later Middle Ages,* Oxford, 1947

W. Harrison, 'The Old House of Correction at Hunt's Bank, Manchester', *TLCAS,* vol. 3, 1885

J. H. Harvey, *Gothic England: a survey of national culture, 1300–1550*, London, 1947

S. Hibbert-Ware, *History of the Foundations in Manchester of Christ's College, Chetham's Hospital and the Free Grammar School*, 3 vols, 2 edn. Manchester, 1848

R. Hollingworth, *Mancuniensis, or, An history of the towne of Manchester, and what is most memorable concerning it*, Manchester, 1839

P. Hosker, 'The Stanleys of Lathom and ecclesiastical patronage in the north-west of England during the fifteenth century', *Northern History*, vol. 18, 1982

H. A. Hudson, 'Warden Huntingdon's Rebus in Manchester Cathedral', *TLCAS*, vol. 30, 1912

H. A. Hudson, 'Notes upon the Huntingdon and Stanley Brasses in Manchester Cathedral', *TLCAS*, vol. 31, 1913

H. A. Hudson, 'A List of the Wardens of the College of Manchester with Remarks upon an early MS. Catalogue and an Early Printed List', *TLCAS*, vol. 33, 1915

H. A. Hudson, *The Mediaeval Woodwork of Manchester Cathedral*, Manchester, 1924

C. Hussey, 'Wenlock Abbey Shropshire – 1', *Country Life*, 1 December 1960

M. K. Jones, and M. G. Underwood, *The King's Mother, Lady Margaret Beaufort Countess of Richmond and Derby*, Cambridge, 1992

T. Kelly, *Early Public Libraries: a History of Public Libraries in Great Britain before 1850*, London, 1966

E. F. Letts, 'Warden Huntyngton', *TLCAS,* vol. 2, 1884

C. Morris, ed., *Illustrated Journeys of Celia Fiennes,* London, 1982

M. Morris, *Medieval Manchester, A Regional Study*, GMAU, 1983

W. Mullis, *A Brief Account of the Blue Coat Hospital and Public Library in The College, Manchester Founded by Humphrey Chetham Esq. In the year 1651*, Manchester, 1826

J. Newman, 'Oxford Libraries before 1800', *Archaeological Journal,* 1978

H. Newcome, *The Diary of the Rev. Henry Newcome from September 20, 1661 to September 29, 1663*, Chetham Society, 1849

A. Nicholson, *The Chetham Hospital and Library,* Manchester, 1910

A. Oswald, 'Chetham's Hospital Furniture', *Country Life* offprint, 25 August and 1 September 1934

Palatine Notebook, vol. 1, 1881

Palatine Notebook, vol. 3, 1883

W. A. Pantin, 'Chantry Priests Houses and other Medieval Lodgings', *Medieval Archaeology,* no. 3, 1959

R. Parkinson, ed., *The Life of Adam Martindale written by Himself,* Chetham Society, 1845

C. T. E. Phillips, 'Humphrey Chetham and his Library', *Manchester Review*, vol. 3, 1944

F. R. Raines, & C. W. Sutton, *The Life of Humphrey Chetham*, 2 vols, Chetham Society, 1903

F. R. Raines, *The Rectors of Manchester and the Wardens of the Collegiate Church of that Town*, Chetham Society, 1885

F. R. Raines, *A History of the Chantries*, Chetham Society, 1862

F. R. Raines, *Notitia Cestriensis or Historical Notices of the Diocese of Chester*, vol. 2, Chetham Society, 1849

M. Rothapel, 'Philanthropy and a Seventeenth Century Charitable Institution in Manchester: A study of Chetham's Hospital 1653–1684', University of Manchester MA thesis, 1998

W. H. Shercliffe, 'Richard Martinscrofte and his Maps', *TLCAS*, vol. 80, 1980

W. J. Smith, *The East Wing, Ordsall Hall, Salford*, GMAU, 1995

T. Stanley Ball, 'Chetham Hospital Silver Plate', *TLCAS*, vol. 26, 1908

J. Stanning, ed., *The Lancashire Royalist Composition Papers*, Record Society of Lancashire and Cheshire, 1892

B. H. Streeter, *The Chained Library: a survey of four centuries in the evolution of the English library*, London, 1931

M. Sykes, 'Pages of History', *Country Life*, 20 January 1983

J. Tait, *Medieval Manchester and the Origins of Lancashire*, Manchester, 1904

H. Taylor, *Old Halls in Lancashire and Cheshire*, Manchester, 1884

L. Toulmin-Smith, *The Itinerary of John Leland in or about the years 1535 to 1543*, London, 1909

I. Tyers, *Tree Ring Analysis of Timbers from Chethams Library and School, Long Millgate, Manchester*, English Heritage, 2002

W. R. Whatton, *A History of Chetham's College and Library*, Manchester, 1833

T. S. Willan, *Elizabethan Manchester*, Chetham Society, Manchester, 1980

M. Wood, *The English Medieval House*, London, 1965

CHETHAM'S LIBRARY

Allen Deeds Parcel N (302) (ii). Letter to Mr Bridoake from Humphrey Chetham, March 17 1648

Allen Deeds Parcel N (299). Money disbursed about the Colledge Business, June 1653 – May 1646

Allen Deeds Parcel S (1). The College in Manchester Survayed by Richard Martinscrofte and others.

Allen Deeds Parcel S (2). Building Accounts July 1656 – April 1658

C/CHL/Min/1–6. Minute Books of the Feoffees, December 1653 – October 1932.

C/COLLEGE/1–29. Deeds, leases, releases and indentures

C/LIB/AC/2ii. Shelf list of 1680 and an inventory of 1671 with amendments of 1681

Grant by letters patent of Edward VI of the College House of Manchester and other property to Edward third Earl of Derby and his heirs, 9 July 1549

GREATER MANCHESTER COUNTY RECORD OFFICE

K1 Plans, measured drawings and perspectives by John Palmer

MANCHESTER CENTRAL LIBRARY

Manchester Deeds L1/51/8/13

J. E. Bailey, ed., *Diary for the Years 1595–1601 of Dr John Dee*, privately printed book, 1880

Index

References in *italic* type include illustrations

69. Asleep at his studies. Early twentieth century slide from the collection at Chetham's Library